Which Equalities Matter?

TO BE
DISPOSED
BY
AUTHORITY

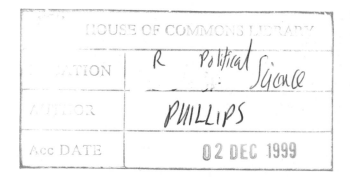

Which Equalities Matter?

Anne Phillips

Polity Press

First published in 1999 by Polity Press
in association with Blackwell Publishers Ltd.

Editorial office:
Polity Press
65 Bridge Street
Cambridge CB2 1UR, UK

Marketing and production:
Blackwell Publishers Ltd
108 Cowley Road
Oxford OX4 1JF, UK

Published in the USA by
Blackwell Publishers Inc.
Commerce Place
350 Main Street
Malden, MA 02148, USA

ISBN 0-7456-2108-2
ISBN 0-7456-2109-0 (pbk)

A catalogue record for this book is available from the British Library.

Typeset in 11 on 13 pt Berling by Wearset, Boldon, Tyne & Wear.
Printed in Great Britain by TJ International, Padstow, Cornwall.

This book is printed on acid-free paper.

Contents

Preface

I wrote this book in response to political and intellectual developments I saw occurring across a number of countries, but it will be apparent to British readers that it is also a more local reaction. The election in 1997 of an economically conservative but constitutionally radical Labour government posed the question of which equalities matter in a particularly stark way. It also put some of us on the defensive about whether to consider ourselves 'old' or 'new'. The choice presented itself: to range oneself with the iconoclasts, with those who had shaken themselves free from the constraints of old labour thinking and had the openness of spirit to question its most foundational assumptions; or to reveal oneself as a backward-looking nostalgic, still seduced by false dreams of economic equality, still warming to the inefficient regimentation of the post-war welfare state. As someone whose political formation had been in feminist challenges to the masculinity of labourist traditions, I felt a curious sense of dislocation in rallying to defend earlier ideals of economic equality against the onslaught of the new. One aim of this book is to challenge the perversity of that either/or choice.

My thanks to David Held for suggesting I write a short, argumentative book just as my thoughts were turning this way, and for his insightful comments on the first draft. John Baker, Nancy Fraser, David Miller, Rosemary Pringle and Iris Young helped as much by their objections as by their support; while Brian Barry provided a characteristically robust reader's report. I enjoyed generous sabbatical leave from London Guildhall University in

1997–8, and am particularly grateful to Iwan Morgan for arranging this.

Special thanks to Ciaran Driver for providing me (yet again) with a title; and to Declan and Mark (Anthony) for so thoughtfully pointing out my inconsistencies when it comes to equality between parents and children.

1
Democracy and Equality

Equality is now off the political agenda; nobody these days believes people can or should be made equal. This is true enough in one sense, very far from true in another. Economic equality has certainly fallen into disuse, tainted as it is by the failures of socialism, and made to seem hopelessly out of kilter with celebrations of diversity and choice. But if some aspects of equality have dropped out of fashion, others have come more prominently to the fore. Equality between the sexes is now considered such a defining characteristic of contemporary (Western) morality that journalists have begun worrying about the horrible effects this is having on the boys; racist classifications and hierarchies have been discredited, if not yet silenced; while the idea that democracies should respect and accommodate minority cultures and practices has come to be regarded as part of the meaning of equal citizenship in a multicultural world. Against this background, it would be absurd to say people have lost interest in equality. The more telling point is that in the weird mix of more with less equality, there has been a parting of the ways between political and economic concerns. It is the separation between these two that lies at the heart of this book.

The separation is particularly marked when you consider the high importance now attached to democracy, and the way that enthusiasm for political equality combines with complete lack of interest in its economic counterpart. One might, I suppose, see the explosion of interest in democracy as a matter more of prudence than of equality: people could be said to favour

democratic forms of government, not because of any grand
commitment to human equality, but simply because these are
safer than the other alternatives. But even if prudential considerations loom large in the justifications for democracy, they have
always combined with deeper assertions about equal worth.
Democracy implies a rough equality between people in their
influence on political affairs, and this expression of political
equality rests on and reinforces profound notions about social
equality. When Jeremy Bentham said that each should count for
one and none for more than one, he did not mean this as a grand
statement about human equality; but this deceptively simple
dictum turned out to convey a daringly egalitarian ideal.
Democracy is never just a system for organizing the election of
governments. It also brings with it a strong conviction about the
citizens being of intrinsically equal worth.

Set alongside the history of man's inhumanity to man, this
statement sounds a long way from what people actually believe,
but as a principle regulating how societies should treat their citizens, it has achieved almost foundational status. We do not have
to defend it by reference to divine injunction or by evidence that
all humans are the same. Equality has become the default position, the principle to which we return when arguments for
inequality have failed. Even the most vigorous defence of
inequality typically starts from some statement of egalitarianism,
employing equality before the law to defend the inequalities of
private property, or equality of opportunity to defend inequalities in income and wealth. Where people continue to promote
institutions premised on social inequality, they usually do so in
terms that pretend the inequality away. Supporters of the British
monarchy, for example, no longer claim that those of royal blood
are 'better' than the rest. They talk, rather, of the monarchy as a
protection against the vicissitudes of parliamentary politics, an
important part of the national heritage, or more simply a tourist
attraction and entertaining show. Arguments premised on social
inequality no longer work. Few now care to defend inequality on
non-egalitarian grounds.

Democracy erodes assumptions of natural superiority, and the
experience of living in even the most enfeebled of democracies
encourages citizens to look askance at privileges of history or
birth. What was once taken for granted comes under closer

scrutiny: in recent years, this has included closer scrutiny not only of the rich and powerful, but of the relationship between the sexes, the unequal treatment of white and black citizens, and the one-sided assimilationism that threatens the integrity of minority cultural groups. Egalitarianism, in this sense, is getting stronger rather than weaker, and its force is the more remarkable when compared with the painfully slow progress of earlier centuries and decades. Political equality was put on the European agenda in seventeenth-century challenges to the powers of hereditary monarchs, and was subsequently extended to query all kinds of pretension based upon birth; it was only, however, with the transition to modern representative democracy that it translated into anything approaching one person, one vote. Nineteenth-century battles over the suffrage whittled away at the property qualifications for citizenship, but voting rights for women were only conceded (with great reluctance and misgivings) in the first half of the twentieth century, and as late as the 1960s, the Southern states of the USA were still denying black people their right to vote. It was not until 1994 that South Africa held its first non-racial elections.

The movement has been bumpy and much contested, and yet there does seem to be a ratchet effect associated with political equality: it is rare for any country that has achieved universal suffrage to go back willingly on this. There are still those who consider men intrinsically superior to women, or regard white people as intrinsically superior to black. There are many who regard the political preferences and judgements of the poor as of negligible account. However pervasive such sentiments, they rarely end up in campaigns to deny the despised ones their political rights, and it is mainly when people have convinced themselves that the others are not 'really' citizens of the same country that disenfranchisement is raised as an issue. The exceptions are important, but the notion that all adults should have the same basic rights is too well established for significant deviation.

The movement, if any, is in the opposite direction, towards making the equality more substantial rather than giving some of it away. Democracy holds out a twin promise of political equality and popular power, and while the practice of actual democracies has been discouraging on both fronts, these promises have continued to fuel activity designed to make reality live up to the ideal. On the political front (in contrast to the economic) this is a period of marked innovation – surprisingly so, perhaps, considering that the world historic victory of liberal democracy was supposed to bring about the 'end of history' and curtail now pointless debates. For a short time at the end of the 1980s, radical democrats were seriously on the defensive. It was bad enough to be troubled by self-doubt, to wonder whether it really made sense to call for a more participatory democracy when everyone around seemed so deeply bored by politics, or whether elite rule was after all inevitable and it was utopian to talk of popular control. Faced with an explosion of explicitly liberal democracies,[1] those dreams became even harder to defend. For a brief moment, it seemed there was nothing more to be said. There was only one kind of democracy, and the majority of the world's countries had come round to adopting it. Radicals regrouped themselves within the broad framework of liberal-representative democracy, abandoned what now seemed the embarrassing opposition between bourgeois and socialist democracy, distanced themselves from traditions of direct or participatory democracy, and quietly made their peace with the duller routines of competitive elections.

The moment of consensus proved, however, only a preamble to renewed discussion of the forms and principles of democracy. Constitution building in Eastern Europe, Latin America and Africa reopened questions about federalism, forms of representation, and the nature of electoral systems that turned out not to be so neatly settled; while in the established democracies, new (as well as some older) questions were raised about the inadequacies of the liberal settlement. Some of the criticisms take up unfinished business that should have been sorted out decades ago. The British election in 1997 brought in an economically conservative but constitutionally radical Labour government. This marked the end of the road for a hereditary House of Lords, set in train the devolution of power to independent assemblies in Scotland and Wales, and raised the real possibility of an alternative to the first-past-the-post system for electing representatives to the House of Commons. The belated acknowledgement that a second chamber composed of hereditary peers is at odds with modern democracy is an obvious example of unfinished business. The introduction of new systems of proportional representation (agreed, at the time of writing, for the Scottish Parliament and Welsh Assembly and looking likely for the House of Commons as well) merely brings Britain into line with the practices of other liberal democracies; while even the more novel arguments that have linked changing the electoral system to raising the proportion of women in politics can be illustrated by reference to near neighbours in other parts of Europe.[2] The attention devoted to constitutional reform none the less marks a new departure in British politics, reflecting widespread disenchantment over a number of years with the institutions of existing democracy.

Other developments have more explicitly challenged dominant conventions of liberal democracy. The revival of civic republicanism (particularly strong in the United States) challenges the proceduralist understanding of democracy as a neutralist shell within which individuals pursue their own private interests and gains, and argues for a politics of strong civic engagement as the condition for free self-government.[3] The literature on deliberative democracy attacks the 'thin' democracy that treats politics as a glorified market, and argues that the quality of democratic decision-making depends on sustained conditions for dialogue, deliberation and talk.[4] In growing contestations around political presence, people have rejected the complacent understanding of political equality as no more than the equal right to vote and stand for election, and argued that the persistent under-representation of women and members of ethnic and racial minorities threatens the democratic validity of decision-making assemblies.[5] Concern with what is perceived as the cultural imperialism of many liberal polities has sparked extensive discussion of the conditions for multicultural citizenship, including whether minority groups might require differential rights and facilities in order to be guaranteed the status of equals.[6] None of these proposes a wholesale dismantling of the practices of liberal-representative democracy: everyone seems to envisage a democracy in which there will continue to be competitive elections, still organized primarily under the umbrella of national parties, still producing a minority who will function as representatives of the rest. All none the less push firmly against the limits of existing practice. New issues then combine with older questions to reopen debates on democracy.

Political equality as a confidence trick?

Democracy is not a new issue. The novelty is the willingness to deal in what previous generations would have disparaged as 'merely' political reforms; and the perception that democracies have failed to deliver even political equality to many of their constituent groups. For much of this century, initiatives to deepen democracy tended to fall into one of two categories. Some looked to alternative political arrangements as a way of achieving more equal and active participation: the decentralization of decision-making; perhaps more decisions taken in mass meetings than by distantly elected representatives; greater use of the referendum or citizen's initiative so as to maximize popular power. Others focused on underlying social and economic arrangements, arguing that people could never be politically equal if they still lived in an unequal world. The self-declared 'realists' went off in a third direction, claiming that any dissonance between ideals and reality merely proved the ideals out of date: if we could just bring ourselves to see that democracy is no more than a novel and convenient way of selecting political elites, we could free ourselves from disabling resentment and the disruptive pursuit of popular power. As far as commonsense understandings are concerned, the realists probably won the day. But for the significant minority that still views democracy as an unfulfilled promise of citizen equality, one recurring question has been whether to prioritize political or economic change. Does the prospect for further democratization depend primarily on the kinds of political or legal arrangement a society adopts? Or do institutional differences fade into irrelevancy when compared with the abolition of private property or initiatives to tackle the unequal distribution of income and wealth?

The answer, almost certainly, lies between these two (we need better institutions *and* more substantive equality) but there has been a powerful strand of thinking through this century that has disparaged any preoccupation with medium-term institutional reform. Marxists, in particular, came to regard political equality almost as a confidence trick, a surface egalitarianism that obscures or legitimates deeper inequalities in social and economic life. In his essay 'On the Jewish Question', Karl Marx argued that the real meaning of political emancipation was the emancipation of civil society *from* the state: a political annulment of distinctions based on birth, rank, education, occupation or religion that freed these distinctions to do whatever they could in the sphere of civil society.[7] The distinction between Jew and Christian was made politically irrelevant, but this did not mean people were emancipated from religion. On the contrary, in the land of the most complete political emancipation (in Marx's view, the United States), religion was more pervasive than ever, almost as if it had received an extra boost from the secular separation of church from state. By the same token, Marx noted, the political annulment of private property (the declaration that all citizens have equal rights regardless of their property status) does not abolish private property. If anything, it frees private, egotistical, property-owning man to wreak whatever havoc he wants in the unbridled regions of civil society. Though Marx claimed to see political emancipation as a big step forward, his support for it only makes sense within a framework that views the heightening of contradictions as the necessary preliminary to further transformation. The essence of his critique is not that political emancipation goes so far but that it does not yet go far enough (always a reasonable enough basis on which to support inadequate initiatives). The problem for Marx is that it actively frees market relationships from the moral constraints that had previously held them in check.

This particular critique of political equality has dulled through subsequent years, for as the possibilities inherent in universal suffrage became more apparent, people employed their newly won political rights to set limits to market egoism and introduce morality into the market sphere. Governments now protect workers from the more excessive demands of their employers, provide a humanitarian safety net that keeps people out of the direst poverty, and impose at least some of the requirements of justice on the operations of the market economy. Marx's conviction that political emancipation would free civil society from politics no longer seems so plausible, and most criticisms of political equality have fallen back on the lesser point that it goes so far but not far enough. For socialists in particular, the operation of the market economy and the nature of capitalist production have been seen as impediments to political equality. Formal equalities mask substantive inequalities, and failing a major

assault on the principles of the market economy, the minority
will hold on to its power. Economic equalization then appears as
the necessary condition for greater political equality.

That revolutionary socialists should see economic inequality as
subverting the pretence of political equality will come as no great
surprise. The more remarkable point is that the economic limits
to democracy were so widely canvassed outside this camp, and
that many of the leading post-war theorists of democracy and citizenship focused on social inequality as the main obstacle to the
development of democratic equality. T.H. Marshall's influential
analysis of the relationship between civil, political and social
rights gave the impression that the battle for civil and political
equality was virtually won (at least in the established democracies), and turned attention to the social rights to employment,
education, or a decent standard of living that Marshall regarded
as necessary to full membership of the citizen community.[8]
Though the conclusions they drew did not usually include a
commitment to welfare reform, much of the work of American
political scientists followed a similar pattern. The major studies
of political participation in the 1960s and 1970s identified the
unequal distribution of political resources as the biggest block to
equal participation in politics; again and again, these turned out
to be a function of the unequal distribution of education and
income.[9] Robert Dahl, once reviled by radicals as the mouthpiece of a complacent pluralism that saw democracy as rule by
elites, has argued that the inequalities generated by market
society are in tension with the promise of political equality, and
has suggested that the next great democratic revolution must
involve significant restrictions on the freedom of the market in
order to address this problem.[10] The notion that political equality
is subverted by the persistence of economic inequalities is not
peculiar to the Marxist tradition.

Across a reasonably wide spectrum of post-war opinion, there
seemed to be a consensus that specifically political reforms had
gone as far as we could expect them to go. We had universal suffrage, regular competitive elections, relatively secure guarantees
regarding freedom of expression and freedom of association. We
clearly lacked the active citizen participation that some have
liked to imagine as part of the practice of Athenian democracy.
Given, however, the size of the modern nation state (and the

fact that, unlike Athens, it recognizes all adults as citizens), we probably had as good a system of political representation and democratic accountability as could be hoped for under current conditions. The results patently failed to deliver either equality of political influence or substantial popular control, but those who worried about this were more likely to focus on underlying social and economic inequalities than put their faith in further programmes of political or constitutional reform. The main exception were the proponents of participatory democracy – who had a few heady years in the 1960s and 1970s – but most of these were also committed to programmes for economic reform. Through much of the second half of the twentieth century, those troubled by the shortcomings in existing democracy have looked to social and economic transformation as the key to fuller equality.

The starting point for this book is that this pattern has now been reversed. Current work on democracy is notable for its pre-occupation with equality in a context of difference: whether equal citizenship for women and men means denying or acknowledging sexual difference; whether equal treatment for minority cultures is compatible with imposing majority practices and norms. Because much of this explores subtler forms of exclusion or disparagement, it has been less focused on economic 'conditions'. Current work is also notable for its interest in institutional and constitutional design: whether the rights and freedoms of citizens are better protected by majority rule or a Bill of Rights interpreted by an independent judiciary; whether electoral systems based on proportionality will be better able to deliver a fair representation of women and a country's ethnic and racial minorities; whether extensive use of the referendum or citizen's initiative endangers minority interests or promotes popular power. Politics, in this sense, has made a come-back. Commenting on the constitutional preoccupations of parties and governments in post-communist Eastern Europe, Claus Offe and Ulrich Preuss note that from the Marxist-Leninist perspective that used to guide these countries, the new emphasis on getting the political institutions right looks like a sad case of putting the cart before the horse.[11] People who used to treat relations of production as determinant and forms of democracy as merely derivative now regard the design of political institutions as decisive in shaping what their countries will become. Meanwhile, in the Western democracies, critiques of 'the system' have become critiques of 'the political system', and the idea that there might be economic conditions for political equality barely gets a mention at all.

Where earlier generations took it for granted that further advances in democracy would involve some modification to market relations and some equalization in economic life (left and right were agreed on this, which is why much of the right was anti-democracy), contemporary democrats are more inclined to bracket the economic questions and focus on political arrangements. This is not a matter of degrees of radicalism, for the traditions I am contrasting are similarly inspired by their visions of what democracy could become and similarly incensed by the inadequacies of current practice. When people debate whether group rights are compatible with individual autonomy, what is necessary to guarantee women's full and equal citizenship, or whether the introduction of deliberative opinion polls will enhance the quality of democracy, it is hardly fair to say they have lost interest in democratic equality. In many ways, indeed, the later preoccupations are more thoroughly egalitarian than the earlier ones, for an earlier focus on class obstacles to democracy has broadened out to address inequalities of sex, race, ethnicity, and the relationship between majority and minority cultures. The implications of political equality are being stretched in new and important directions – and yet in the explorations of what it means to treat people as political equals (now including what it means to treat women as equals or what equal citizenship means in societies that are multicultural), the notion that economic equality might be one of the conditions has largely dropped from view. This is the observation that prompts this book. What can be done to deepen and extend democracy is very much on the agenda. The idea that any of this depends on economic equality barely gets a look-in today.

Economic displacement

There is an obvious enough explanation for this, for the last decades of the twentieth century have seriously dented confidence in radical economic reform. A major contributor here is the crisis of socialism, the collapse of the self-styled communist regimes of Eastern Europe and the Soviet Union, and the associated disillusionment with the socialist project in political movements of the Western world. Despite an explicit anti-statism in the works of the founding fathers, the idea that the state should take over from a chaotic and exploitative market had emerged as one of the main themes of the socialist tradition, and the equation between state/good, market/bad had become one of the markers of socialist thought. Hardly anyone these days goes along with that categorization. Most now view the market as playing a central role in the organization of production and distribution; most seem to regard state planning as a hazardous enterprise, likely to do as much harm as good. In my view, the pendulum has swung too far in favour of the entrepreneur as the source of all innovation and energy, and I anticipate considerable correction over future years as it becomes clear that markets can make horrendous mistakes. But even anticipating some reversal, it is harder to feel confident about ways of making people economically equal. Everyone now knows that nationalized industries can become stultified and inefficient, that initiatives to end poverty can end up condemning people to a poverty trap, that when public authorities set out to protect employees' wages and conditions from the harsher realities of the market they often do this at the expense of good service provision. We have even discovered, to our dismay, that the free health and education that was the great achievement of the welfare system can end up redistributing wealth from the poor to the middle classes.[12] With the best will in the world, programmes for redistributive justice often backfire. Since we can no longer pretend to confidence about what makes people economically equal, it is hardly surprising that so many have turned their attention elsewhere.

The other obvious enough point is that the connections previously made between economic and political equality were eased by a widespread belief that societies were moving towards greater equity in the distribution of income and wealth. For the developed world at least, the twentieth century seemed to be bringing about a slow but progressive narrowing of the gap between richest and poorest. It seemed plausible enough to think that most would end up in the middle, with just a sprinkling of super-rich and super-poor. When this was the background belief, it made sense to conceive of democracy as starting a process that would end with economic convergence. Social inequalities propelled people into battle, convincing them that they needed political equality so as to protect their interests; however formal the achievements of this political equality, the majority would use their power to promote majority well-being. The predicted results have been slow in coming, and their progress has been punctuated by repeated worries about working-class deference or media manipulation or successful policies of divide and rule. So long, however, as the figures indicated some narrowing of the gap between rich and poor, this benign reading of the relationship between political and economic equality seemed reasonably plausible. Now that the gap is widening again, those connections look more tenuous.

Many have criticized the widening gap in post-tax incomes. Many more have taken it as a signal that economic egalitarianism is a dead-end project. Politicians who once placed themselves on opposite ends of the political spectrum now seem united in their defence of wide-ranging income differentials and their condemnation of 'simple' or 'levelling' equality, while the notion that justice requires equal shares for all is regarded as so simpleminded that no-one can believe equality was ever intended so literally. Even the more modest principle of universal entitlement to public services and state benefits is frequently presented as an anachronism. What is the point, people ask, of employing public resources to fund free education or free health when the richer members of society are only too happy to pay for higher standards of provision than can be made available to the average citizen? What is the good, others go on to enquire, of employing public resources to target the poorer members of society if this only generates a 'dependency culture' that prevents people looking for work? Universal entitlement is presented as unnecessary because the rich don't need it and inappropriate because it drags them down. But the means-tested targeting of the poor is also criticized as an inappropriate way of dealing with poverty, for it is said to promote a dependency on state handouts that encourages people to abdicate responsibility for their lives.

In both these arguments, an earlier discourse of economic egalitarianism has given way to a new emphasis on individual responsibility. Extremes of income and wealth are no longer presented as undesirable in themselves. The only undesirable element is that they may lock certain members of society into an inability to take care of themselves. The state then has a responsibility to ensure that opportunities for self-advancement are made equally available to every citizen, an obvious responsibility in the fields of education and training, with perhaps some additional responsibilities to assist lone parents back into the labour market, or to make the feckless take out insurance policies to protect them from future disaster. Since the state raises its money through taxation, there will continue to be a redistributive element in this: no one has the nerve to say the poor should pay as much in taxes as the rich, though in practice they often pay proportionately more. But even those on the left of the political spectrum no longer seem to look to the state to equalize material conditions. The equalization is to be in opportunities for self-advancement, not in levels of income and wealth.

The retreat from economic egalitarianism has had its effect on the way democracy is discussed, and it is hardly surprising that we now hear less about the incompatibility between capitalism and democracy or the illusory nature of political equality in an unequal world. But the causality can also work the other way. It may be that changes in the way democracy is discussed have affected attitudes towards economic equality, and that the retreat from economic egalitarianism has been assisted by new ways of thinking about political equality. This is one of the issues I address. I do not go along with those who say that the energy now devoted to sexual or racial equality has diverted attention from more 'fundamental' economic inequalities, or that a new preoccupation with multiculturalism and identity politics has disrupted previous solidarities based on class.[13] But I cannot avoid troubled thoughts about the way developments I otherwise support have contributed (however inadvertently) to a declining interest in economic equality. In her analysis of the US left, Nancy Fraser has written of a tension between redistribution and recognition, a tension, that is, between an older politics that draws on socialist critiques of the capitalist economy and a later one that deals with the recognition claims of identity groups. She notes that the current preoccupation with cultural domination seems to be crowding out economic injustices.[14] I see a similar process at work in the literature on democracy, where important new issues about citizenship and difference crowd out older questions of economic equality.

As far as debates on democracy are concerned, the most notable recent developments have been (1) the heightened interest in institutional and constitutional design; (2) the shift of attention from the class inequalities that undermine democracy to the gender, racial or cultural hierarchies that subvert equal citizenship; (3) the new preoccupation with equality under conditions of difference. I discuss in the next chapter what I take to be the importance of these developments, and merely note at this stage that they have illuminated much unfinished business around civil and political equality, exposed political/cultural mechanisms of group exclusion, and made empowerment a more central concern. The broadening out of the remit of democracy has made it possible to identify forms of domination that were not previously regarded as political: the viciousness of domestic violence and racial assaults; the demonization of Islam; the crippling self-hatred that can be imposed on people whose cultural values are socially despised. This has generated debate over the implications of ethical pluralism, and whether it is legitimate to think of democracies as pursuing 'a common good' when their citizens may hold such diverse religious and ethical views. It has also raised important questions about the meaning of equality in a world of difference, and whether one should conceive of political equality as a relationship between those who are different rather than an attempt to make them the same.

The shift of perspective that has allowed these issues to emerge has, in my view, been immensely fruitful. But something rather odd has happened en route. Inequalities that can no longer be regarded as exclusively economic are treated as if they are not at all so, while economic changes that can only partially address a problem are treated as if they are entirely irrelevant. It is as if one is required to choose between politics and economics. Either one treats the deepening of equality as wholly dependent on cultural initiatives, political empowerment, better institutional design; or one goes back to an earlier tradition that concentrated exclusively on social and economic reform. It is as if the economic conditions for democracy can only be taken seriously when they are regarded as both necessary and sufficient. Once admit that there are other conditions, and we can forget any economic concerns.

Remaking connections

My perception of current debates is not, as it happens, that there has been a deliberate turn away from the relationship between political and economic equality, or much explicit argument about what can be done through politics alone. David Marquand, to give one example, argues that prominent thinkers in post-war Britain assumed too readily that civil and political rights were secure, and that with the first two floors of citizenship already in place, democratic socialists could concentrate their energies on promoting greater social and economic equality. This assumption, he suggests, was mistaken. 'Perhaps Marshall, Crosland and those who thought like them had tried to build the top floor of citizenship before the first two floors were in place. And if that were true, the obvious conclusion was that the struggle for political citizenship which the post-war generation had assumed to be over, would have to be waged anew.'[15] Marquand here makes an argument in favour of returning to the political front, but as the rest of his work makes clear, this is because he believes that only an empowered and active citizenry can make any further progress towards social equality. The turn towards politics need not (in my argument, should not) lead people away from matters of social and economic concern. Yet in practice, discussions of civic republicanism or cultural pluralism or equal citizenship for women and men often proceed as if these had nothing to do with economic arrangements or the distribution of income and wealth. In the context of an unequal world, this has to be regarded as an implausible assumption.

It is the relationship between political and economic equality that is at the core of this book: political equality understood not only as the equal right to participate in politics but as that deeper notion of equal intrinsic worth; economic equality understood as equality in income, wealth, and life-chances, and including access to socially provided resources such as education or health. Political equality suggests what Robert Dahl calls a 'roughly equal qualification' for government,[16] but this only makes sense if we think people really are equal in some important way. It is that assertion about a fundamental human equality (in the capacity for reason, or perhaps just capacity for suffering) that underpins my use of the term. The development of democracy is never just about the introduction of a certain kind of franchise; it rests on and encourages the development of a democratic political culture that comes to interpret political equality in a much broader way. I employ political equality in this wider sense, encompassing then what others have described as social or cultural equality. Because of this, I regard the term as inevitably open-ended. Debates about democracy are always, in part, discussions of what political equality means and how far it should be taken. In this sense, it is not something that can be defined in advance.

Economic equality also eludes prior definition, and I discuss in chapter 3 some of the difficulties in establishing what it means. One of the shadows that hangs over this discussion is the resignation (by all except some fragments of the left) to the persistence of capitalism. There used to be quite a lively debate between those who thought of inequality in terms of distribution and those who thought of it in terms of production, the former dealing in quantifiable levels of income and wealth, the latter in the power relations that expose workers to the commands of employers, subject them to exploitation, and alienate them from the very labour that could be giving meaning to their lives. Considered in the first way – as the distribution of income and wealth – economic inequality falls into the realm of something that can be ameliorated if not totally eliminated, for even if we leave the structure of production relatively intact, it is possible to tax the wealthy and use the proceeds to raise the incomes of the poor. Considered as a deeper matter of capital's power over labour, there is not much to be done by fiddling around with income differentials or equalizing post-tax wealth. While capitalism remains, there will still be a problem of inequality: first, because capitalism depends on profits and cannot accommodate significant redistribution; secondly, because it requires capital to retain command over labour, which necessarily means unequal power.

In an era that sees no viable alternative to capitalism, this last is a deeply uncomfortable conclusion. Hardly anyone nowadays anticipates eliminating the market, abolishing private property, ending alienated work, or overcoming the division between mental and manual labour. We still argue about the balance between public and private ownership or how much governments should interfere with the operations of the market, and we can certainly identify different kinds of capitalism, some more hospitable to equality than others. Few, however, expect to eliminate (as opposed to ameliorating) structural inequalities embedded in capitalist production. Since I share this view, I see little to be gained from establishing the incompatibility between capitalist relations of production and political equality. Nothing (beyond an acute attack of depression) would follow from this. The more immediate questions relate to inequalities over which societies can claim some control, and for this reason, I focus largely on distributional questions. When I talk of economic inequality, I refer primarily to the unequal distribution of life-chances, income and wealth. This distribution is also, of course, structural, for individuals are born into pre-existing positions in a social and economic hierarchy and the structures they enter will significantly shape their future lives. (They are born to rich parents or poor, for example; they are born male or female in societies that still load this with meaning for their future responsibilities and roles.) Focusing on distribution rather than production does not mean focusing on individual rather than structural inequality. It only means that I set aside some of the more intractable problems associated with wage labour and commodity production.

I also set aside important questions about the way conditions of corporate capitalism constrain the exercise of popular control, making the supposed freedom and equality of citizens a desperately unbalanced affair. 'Democracy', as David Held puts it, 'is embedded in a socio-economic system that grants a "privileged position" to certain interests.'[17] The point here is not just that the wealthy find it easier to disseminate their views, to finance newspapers, launch pressure groups, lunch prime ministers. More troubling (because more systemic) is the fact that all governments depend on the process of capital accumulation as the source of incomes, growth, and jobs, and must therefore ensure that the economic policies they pursue do not undermine the prosperity of the private sector. This structural privileging of corporate power means that the democratic playing field is never level. Even if one imagines a situation where all citizens enjoy the same social status, the same (real) opportunities for political participation, and the same chance of making their voices heard, the political agenda will still be biased in advance.

In what follows, I have little to say on the exercise of power by private corporations, or the way this constrains popular control. Initiatives to strengthen democratic control over corporate power are an important part of the project of democracy, but are not my main concern. My primary focus is on what democracy suggests about the relationship between citizens, and the promise it holds out (but on which it so rarely delivers) about our status as political equals. In the framework of a culturally plural world, I see the furthering of that equality as requiring a new relationship between majority and minority cultures, and a new settlement between women and men. But in the context of what remains an economically unequal world, I also see it as intimately bound up with reducing income differentials and reforming the division of labour. In what follows, I take issue with the retreat from economic egalitarianism that characterizes so much thinking in academic and popular debate.

In chapter 2 I set out more fully what I see as the main features in a left 'turn towards politics'. That the right should have abandoned economic equality is hardly surprising; the surprise is that so little is now said from the centre or the left. Part, at least, of the explanation for this is the left's preoccupation with what has come to be described as a politics of difference and/or a politics of recognition: the idea that liberal democracy has repressed recognition of differences by gender, ethnicity, race, religion, language or culture, and that this repression means people are not being treated as equals. I defend this politics of difference against some of the more common criticisms levelled at it (mostly to the effect that we should treat people as individuals and not as members of some group). I also, however, see it as contributing to the separation of political from economic equality.

Chapter 3 addresses recent debates over the nature and meaning of economic equality and asks whether economic equality matters in itself, regardless of its impact on political equality. If it does not matter, then my anxieties are clearly misplaced.

Why worry about severing the link between politics and economics if there are no independent reasons for favouring greater economic equality? Though I come to the conclusion that strict equality is neither coherent nor morally required, I argue that the recent retreat from economic egalitarianism is misplaced and the proposed alternatives unconvincing.

Chapter 4 argues that the commitment to political equality gives new urgency and importance to the case for economic equality, and that this is particularly so because of what is implied in recognizing other citizens as one's equals. It then goes on to ask what happens to such arguments in the movement from a class-defined analysis of inequality to one that focuses on differences by gender, ethnicity or race. One of the central issues here is whether the critique of assimilationism (the one-way assimilation of group X into group Y's norms) can be detached from a critique of convergence. Do contemporary arguments about securing equality *through* difference mean that no significance should be attached to convergence in economic and social conditions? Or are certain kinds of difference still incompatible with political equality, and does this restore the connections between political and economic equality?

This deals with one perennial critique of democracy: that it uncouples political from economic equality, leaving us with no more than a 'formal' equality. The other widely voiced criticism comes in from the opposite direction, and it is to this I turn in chapter 5. Liberal democracy is often said to turn politics into the handmaiden of interest, reducing the activities of citizenship to little more than the protection of individual and group self-interest. This can be read as a critique of the unequal society, for if society were not divided into large and contesting interest groups, we might have a better chance of developing a politics that resonated with justice or addressed itself to matters of common concern. Those who look to the resuscitation of a more public-spirited democracy often start from this. But because they are particularly exercised by what they see as the narrow preoccupations of interest-group politics, they also tend to exclude expressions of interest from the political domain. In the framework of an unequal society, this has the effect of confirming many of the inequalities they sought to contest.

2
Taking Difference Seriously

The transformations of recent decades reflect a negative experience of socialist collapse: the rightwards shift in the political consensus, and delighted abandonment of issues of economic equality. On the left, the changes reflect more positive developments: the anti-racism that developed so powerfully from the civil rights movement in the USA; the resurgence of feminism through the 1960s and 1970s; the more confident insistence on the rights of minority groups in what are increasingly accepted as multi-ethnic, multicultural societies. Through much of the twentieth century, inequality was understood as a primarily class phenomenon, something associated with the distribution of income and wealth and the effects of private property. Inequalities between male and female, between white and black, or between one country and another also generated important political movements, and it would be poor history to suggest that these inequalities were only recently discovered. But through an era dominated by the big 'capitalism versus socialism' question, inequality had an inescapably class dimension and equality was conceived as a substantially economic affair. Subsequent developments have significantly modified this. One consequence is that equality is now thought to be a matter of politics or culture as much as (if not more than) one of the distribution of economic resources. Another is that difference has begun to displace inequality as the dominant concern of progressive politics.

On the face of it, the revival of feminism and anti-racism hardly explains a movement from economic towards political issues, for the position of women and members of ethnic or racial minorities is very much bound up with economic indicators, and problems of unemployment, poverty, or low pay have figured prominently in the political movements associated with these groups. The shift from a predominantly class understanding of inequality to one that focuses on gender, ethnicity and race none the less forced a reassessment of achievements in that 'merely' political field, bringing issues of civil and political equality more prominently to the fore. As its name suggests, the civil rights movement exposed the complacency of those who thought that civic and political equality had already been achieved, and that the only outstanding problems were those associated with economic inequality. As late as the 1960s, African Americans still lacked the political rights of suffrage, and were still being denied what should have been the basic civil right to travel freely on public transport or eat in the restaurant of their choice. One of the successes of that movement was the passage of the 1965 Voting Rights Act that guaranteed the equal right to register and vote; one of the effects of that legislation was that it created a framework within which to campaign for more minority representatives in legislative chambers. The meaning of political equality was extended to include the equal right to elect a representative of one's choice, and this right was increasingly interpreted as the right of minority citizens to be represented by minority politicians. No longer regarding political equality as a simple function of economic equality (something that could only be further advanced by changes in the economic structure), many then turned to the politics of redrawing constituency boundaries so as to raise the proportion of black and Latino representatives.

Similar developments can be tracked in the politics of contemporary feminism. In the early years of the contemporary women's movement, much of the activity was devoted to women's economic situation: supporting strikes for equal pay, campaigning for better employment protection for part-time women workers, or for the childcare provision that would enable women to re-enter the labour market. But much was also devoted to the misrepresentations of women in the media, the sexual harassment of women, the denial of their independent capacity to take out mortgages or sign hire-purchase agreements, the bullying and violence of their husbands, or the patronage visited on women in political meetings and parties. Despite their formation in a counter-cultural movement that despised the conventions of establishment politics, feminists eventually turned their attention to women's exclusion from the conventional political arena, and increasing numbers of political parties have been pressured into adopting measures of affirmative action to secure the election of more women representatives. Though some have derided this as capitulation to a more moderate 'liberal' feminism, it is better understood as part of a reassessment of citizenship that has queried the supposed achievements within the political realm. Where earlier generations had given the impression that all was now fine on the political front (women did, after all, have the right to vote) but pretty depressing in social and economic life, contemporary feminists have argued that sexual inequality pervades the very definitions and practices of politics as well as the conditions of economic life. It is not just that those fine-sounding civil or political equalities are superimposed on deeper social and economic inequalities. There is an important sense in which women have not been recognized as civic and political equals.

Specifically political issues then came to occupy a more central place on the radical agenda. Much of the earlier literature had focused on the gap between formal and substantive equality. This suggested that individuals were indeed recognized as equals, enjoying the same political and civil rights, but were obstructed in the equal deployment of these rights by background conditions relating to social and economic inequality. Though obviously intended to challenge the self-image of democratic societies, even this now appears unduly complacent. Quite apart from the overt inequalities that have persisted in supposedly democratic societies (the denial of political and civil rights to African Americans, the anachronism of the House of Lords), the conventional understanding of equal citizenship also skews matters in favour of dominant groups. The formal equality is wanting, well before we address substantive conditions.

Equality and difference

The central theme that has developed in discussions of this is the relationship between equality and difference. Feminist analyses of the liberal democratic tradition have drawn attention to the way seemingly innocent notions of freedom, equality or consent were founded on an equation between the citizen and the male. This was most apparent in the formative literature of the sixteenth and seventeenth centuries, where exciting new ideas about government being based on consent were welded on to less thrilling ideas about men as the 'natural' heads of their households, and the emerging discourse of free self-government came to be premised on sexual subordination. Similar deformations have continued right through the twentieth century. The rights of citizenship have been variously associated with the responsibility to fight for the defence of one's country, or the dignities and responsibilities of labour (both defined very much out of a masculine experience); and as late as the 1970s, one still finds political theorists writing as if the individual is a male head of household, whose rights can be discussed in abstraction from gender relations.[1]

Left to itself, such evidence of male preferentialism might point towards a more genuine gender-neutrality that no longer discriminates between the two sexes. In much of the feminist literature, however, the critique of male bias has been combined with a more challenging argument that treats gender-neutrality itself as the culprit. All democracies now present themselves as indifferent to sexual difference, proclaiming their citizenship as equally available to both women and men. This very indifference is part of the problem. 'To become a citizen is to trade one's particular identity for an abstract, public self',[2] and this trade-in can be said to be peculiarly advantageous to men. Consider the different balances men and women have had to strike between their public and private lives, and the far greater ease with which men detach themselves (both practically and emotionally) from their private or domestic concerns. In the 'male' norm of democratic politics, the boundaries between public and private worlds are relatively well policed, and those who stray across these boundaries (taking their babies to political meetings, letting their emotions 'intrude' on rational debate) will be regarded as disruptive or peculiar, as failing to abide by the standards of democratic life. These standards are of course presented as neutral – the same criticisms would apply equally to a woman or a man – but since social characteristics *are* gendered, what passes for neutrality turns out to be preferential treatment for men.

Under the banner of gender-neutrality, sex would have to be treated as an irrelevant consideration. One consequence is that it would be difficult to argue for affirmative action policies designed to raise the proportion of women elected as political representatives: if sex is meant to be irrelevant, why should it matter whether our representatives are women or men? In a world that is patently not neutral between the sexes, proclamations of gender-neutrality then have the effect of affirming the status quo. We carry on with business as usual, which means carrying on with politics monopolized by men. Under the banner of gender-neutrality, it also becomes difficult to tackle deep-rooted assumptions about the nature of justice and rights. One argument developed by feminists is that the ethic of impartial justice needs to be supplemented by an ethic of responsibility or care, and that the impersonal implementation of abstract rules of justice can make us less attentive than we should be to the concrete circumstances of different people's lives and the responsibilities we owe to others.[3] It is probably a mistake to equate the 'ethics of justice' with men and the 'ethics of care' with women, but there is an important gender component here and easy proclamations of gender-neutrality make it harder to get at the issues.

Feminists have taken issue with supposedly sex-blind versions of equality that require women to simulate the activities of the men who constructed these norms. Black activists have developed similar arguments against the race-blindness that makes equality depend on simulating the language and conventions of those who are white.[4] When people have been denied jobs, education or housing because they are black, it does of course seem right that employers or landlords should be required to ignore the skin colour of applicants and block out the 'accidents' of ethnicity or race. But that kind of race-blindness can also be deeply insulting. It gives the impression that racial identity is incidental to an individual's sense of self; worse still, it can send a message about 'blackness' being a problem, something others will live with only when they are able to pretend it away. The suggestion that white is normal and black an unhappy deviation is part of what has been challenged in recent decades.

Despite overtly good intentions, the notion that we make people equal by ignoring or suppressing their difference easily turns into a statement of inequality: a bit like saying 'I regard you as my equal *despite* your peculiarities, despite those surface characteristics that mark you as my inferior.' The idea that equality depends on everyone being treated the same can also be regarded as an inequitable assimilationism that imposes the values and norms of one group on those who were historically subordinate. Consider the much discussed example from Canadian politics, which arose when the prime minister, Pierre Trudeau, decided to tackle the unequal status of indigenous peoples by dismantling the reservation system that had protected the First Nations from assimilation.[5] The reservation system enabled native Indians to retain control over reservation lands, setting limits to the mobility, residence and voting rights of non-Indians in Indian territory. But when the majority of Indians still lived in (impoverished) separate reserves, this also limited their participation in mainstream Canadian life. The government concluded that 'separate but equal' was no guarantee of equality and – in an impeccably liberal move – decided to abandon all differential legislation and treatment. What looked like neutrality was, however, perceived as imposition, and the policy was withdrawn six months later in the face of almost unanimous Indian opposition.

Representatives of indigenous peoples have criticized the assimilationism that requires all peoples to conform to the constitutional preferences of the victorious settlers, and have argued for forms of self-government that will respect traditional practices and customs rather than imposing another group's norms. In similar fashion, migrant communities have sometimes looked askance at the legal equalities that promise identical treatment regardless of one's culture or religion, arguing that exceptions should be made in respect of particular practices that are embedded in the traditions of their group. The resulting emphasis on equality *through* difference is probably the most distinctive feature of contemporary thinking on democracy. The idea that equality requires us all to be the same has long been considered a breach of individuality, and the depressing conformism associated with this was challenged more than a century ago by John Stuart Mill. The idea that equality means treating everyone the same has survived for much longer, as has the related idea that equality is to be promoted by eliminating at least some of the differences.

When class was the paradigmatic example of inequality, the notion that equality meant bracketing out or else getting rid of difference seemed more plausible than it does today. One can treat workers and capitalists as equals by discounting the difference between them (what Marx described and criticized as the political annulment of difference). This is what is supposed to happen in the law courts or in the allocation of the same number of votes to each. Or one can go beyond the traditionally liberal understanding of equality to attack differences themselves: abolish private property, abolish the distinction between capitalist and worker, abolish those differences that just can't be discounted, and then let us talk of equality. Difference, in either case, is treated as a problem. In the first scenario, differences in status have to be ignored in order to guarantee people their equal civil and political rights. In the second, they have to be eliminated in order to make people genuine equals. The disagreement is about how much has to be changed in order to prevent difference having its deleterious effect.

Once attention shifts to other forms of group difference that are not so amenable to erasure, it becomes less appropriate to treat difference as always and inevitably a problem. It is clearly inappropriate to make sexual equality depend on sex-change operations that convert all the men to women or all the women to men, or to make racial equality depend on mass programmes of racial intermarriage that produce a uniform world population. And if those differences must remain – must be made in some way compatible with equality – why should it be so difficult to articulate a vision of equal citizenship that is premised on continuing differences in culture and practices and beliefs? As many now argue, treating people as equals does not have to mean treating them the same; indeed, when treating people the same means subjecting everyone to the norms and institutions that were developed by only one of many groups, this is the opposite of equal treatment. These considerations draw us back (rightly, in my view) into unfinished business around the nature of equal citizenship. It is not just that political equality is being subverted by economic inequality. We need a more adequate understanding of political and civil equality that recognizes and respects our differences.

It may be, to give one widely discussed example, that equality of citizenship requires different groups of people to have different kinds of rights. Legal exemptions that recognize valued practices within minority communities are reasonably commonplace in modern democracies: in Britain, the exemption of Sikh men from legislation compelling all motorcyclists to wear safety helmets, or the exemption of Jewish and Muslim abattoirs from some of the legislation regulating the slaughter of animals. What of more troubling cases, like exemptions from laws banning clitoridectomy or polygamy? Does equal citizenship depend on all citizens being subject to the same civil codes and identical structures of government? Or does it depend on a wider diversity of institutional arrangements that can promote the collective goals of linguistic or cultural communities, or give substantive recognition to the claims of cultural minorities and indigenous peoples? Once we move beyond the simpler reaches of the suffrage – where it may seem obvious enough that treating people as equals means giving them exactly the same number of votes – the precise meaning of political equality is not transparent. Despite the usual formulations of anti-discrimination law, it is not obvious that political and legal arrangements should always be premised on identical treatment, regardless of sex, race, religious beliefs or cultural traditions: that it should never be legitimate to practise affirmative action on behalf of groups who were historically subordinate; or never appropriate to exempt certain groups from regulations imposed on all others. In some contexts identical treatment is right, in others it will make people less equal, and there are difficult questions still to be answered about what falls into each category. One of the benefits of the current turn towards politics is that these tricky questions are more widely acknowledged.

The other question that is more easily raised is whether tolerating people's peculiarities really counts as equal treatment. Liberal democracies have tended to treat equal respect as a

matter of leaving people free to do as they wish in their private
domain, respecting them their privacy, but always on the understanding that their strange practices or beliefs should not intrude
too prominently into public life. A good liberal would want to
decriminalize homosexuality, guarantee the freedom of religion,
protect the civic rights of linguistic minorities; and would adopt
a strong stance of tolerance towards practices she personally
regarded as distasteful so long as these did not interfere with the
freedoms of other citizens. But the tolerance that depends on
keeping one's head down can be viewed as inequitable (why are
some groups allowed to flaunt their practices in public while
others have to keep them to themselves?), and does not do much
to address the basis on which a group has found itself disparaged
or despised. One early defence of homosexuals turned on the
notion that people were simply born that way, and that it made
no more sense to lock people up for their sexuality than to lock
them up for being born with an extra toe. A related defence of
religious dissidents turned on the notion that beliefs are not
beliefs if they can be changed at will, and that while governments can shut down churches or ban what they see as heretical
practices, they cannot seriously expect to 'make' people true
believers. Both arguments have proved reasonably effective in
promoting more liberal legislation and practice, but neither
bothers to question whether the deviants really are so weird.
Maybe, by implication, we should regard homosexuals with fear
and distaste; maybe the religious dissidents really are benighted,
superstitious, heading for the torments of hell. If they can't be
changed they must be accommodated: this is as far as the
argument goes.

  Tolerance of this sort can easily coexist with ignorance and can
certainly coexist with contempt. Those who have agreed to tolerate may feel themselves absolved from any further moves
towards better understanding; and since majority groups rarely
conceive of themselves as requiring equal doses of tolerance from
the minority, they may come to wear their toleration as an additional badge of superiority. The 'live and let live' strategy then
looks profoundly inequitable, and threatens to leave the bases for
intolerance untouched. The alternative strategy (underlying
much recent identity politics) has looked towards recognition
rather than tolerance, and has attached as much weight to public

activities and contestations as to the protections of the private sphere. Sometimes the main objective is challenging stereotypical distortions: getting people to see that one group's practices are no more peculiar than any other's, or that the newspapers have misrepresented a particular group's characteristics or beliefs. Where such initiatives are successful, they can dissolve the very need for tolerance by dissolving the initial suspicions or distaste. At other times, the movement 'beyond tolerance' involves a public affirmation and celebration of differences even to the point where stereotypes may be gleefully reclaimed. If we consider the impact of gay pride marches, for example, we can see both elements at work together. Some of the impact comes from the fact that such a cross-section of society participates in the marches and that gays and lesbians then turn out to be not so very different after all. But much of it comes from the extravagant 'camping up', the celebration and exaggeration of difference, the refusal to keep peculiarities behind closed doors. Where calls for greater tolerance might minimize the impact of any proposed change (this won't really affect you, you'll hardly notice they are there), calls for recognition often insist on the qualities that make people so different and distinct. Equality then becomes more than an accommodation or *modus vivendi*. It means being able to see people as both different *and* equal. It also means recognizing that what we term 'the public' is made up of many different groups.

Raising the stakes from toleration to recognition could, of course, produce a more *in*tolerant society, generating a backlash against 'uppity' minorities and increasing the hostility towards minority groups. People who happily tolerate their unassuming gay neighbour may object strongly to educational programmes that encourage pupils to regard homosexuality as an equally legitimate sexual choice; while those who couldn't care less about their neighbours' religious practices or beliefs may become overtly antagonistic if their government decides to fund separate religious schools. The use of differential rights to protect minority cultural traditions raises difficult questions, and so too does the idea that societies can abandon the 'lesser' reaches of tolerance for the fuller egalitarianism of recognition.[6] I discuss some of the standard liberal objections later in the chapter. The point I stress here is simply that democracies should be prepared to debate these issues, and that a tradition which took social and economic equality as the condition for 'genuine' political equality made it hard even to formulate the questions. One of the benefits of the current politics of difference is that such issues are more widely discussed.

The power of politics

When differences are located in a political, cultural, or legal domain, it is apparent enough that societies can revisit their political or legal arrangements in order to address the resulting inequalities. Political and legal arrangements have also come to the fore as a way of addressing inequalities more obviously situated in social and economic life; and here, too, difference has become central to the debate. This is the second point I want to stress: that even when inequalities are closely bound up with social and economic conditions, it is through politics we make a difference. I do not just mean that we have to act and therefore have to be political. My point, rather, is that where inequalities are bound up with group difference, political (and legal) arrangements can have considerable remedial force. Political reforms cannot substitute entirely for economic and social ones, but can certainly provide the enabling conditions.

In the context of an unequal society – and with the aim of making it more equal – we seem to face one of two choices. We can say that political equality is good but limited, and concentrate our energies on making people economically equal. If we choose this course of action we will have little time to waste on campaigning against political abuses or political inequalities, for we will regard these as the inevitable consequence of an unequal distribution of economic power. Attack the cause not the symptom – or to put it in terms popularized by generations of Marxists, don't go for the superstructure but straight for the base. The other approach sees political equality as a way of countering structural inequalities, and looks to it to compensate for social and economic inequalities. Anyone who argues for the specific representation of marginalized groups or supports quota systems to remedy the under-representation of women and ethnic minorities is opting for this second line of action. She may or may not regard these measures as solving all problems; she is certainly saying much can be done through political arrangements while pending more thorough-going equalization in social life.

There are three good reasons for pursuing this second course. The first is that the empowerment of the currently disadvantaged is often a prerequisite for, rather than a consequence of, more equitable social policies, for until people become active participants in the policy process, the policies adopted cannot be expected to reflect their needs. This is part of what David Marquand means when he says that the struggle for political citizenship has to be waged anew, and that only a more active and empowered citizenry is going to be able to promote greater social equality. It is also what lies at the heart of current discussions about including previously marginalized minority groups, where the recognition of radical plurality and commitment to giving all groups a political voice has become a major theme. The second (more pragmatic) reason is that the culture of liberal democracy is more responsive to pressures for political than economic equalization, and that it is proving easier to persuade people to act against a demonstrated political inequity than against an economic one. The third (perhaps less an argument than an expression of impatience) is simply that people are fed up with waiting for 'more fundamental' social change.

One of the key arguments in Iris Young's *Justice and the Politics of Difference*[7] is that normative political theory has tended to treat questions of social justice as a matter of what people have rather than what they do. Against this, Young makes the empowerment of hitherto oppressed groups the predominant issue. In her analysis, the search for the correct principles of distribution (often conceived as a process of rational enquiry that each individual can pursue on her own) generates a politics from on high, a politics without the politics, in which different social groups play no part in defining the principles of justice. Young argues that such an approach skews the results of the enquiry, delivering us to an idealist fiction that represents the partial preoccupations of currently dominant groups as the last word in impartial, general interest. The alternative is to start from a rigorous understanding of the heterogeneous nature of the contemporary public. Correct principles of justice can only be arrived at when all social groups, including those currently excluded, marginalized and oppressed, are enabled to participate in the formulation of such principles.

Policies on affirmative action, to give one obvious example, will look different from different perspectives, and what is considered economically equitable is likely to vary between those groups who have been historically excluded from certain types of employment and those who have enjoyed a previous monopoly. The empowerment of the currently oppressed then appears as the first necessity, for failing that empowerment, what counts as economic equality or economic justice will be what makes sense to already dominant groups. It is not that empowerment matters more than economic equality, or that democracy has become more important than having enough to eat. The point, rather, is that there is no impartial 'view from nowhere' from which the great social theorists – or not-so-great politicians – can deduce what ought to be done. Young then proposes special representation rights for oppressed groups: public funding to enable them to meet together and formulate their ideas; the right to generate their own policy proposals that would have to be considered by decision-makers; and veto powers for oppressed groups over matters that are most directly their concern.

Though less concerned with the specific institutional arrangements, Jürgen Habermas pursues a related line of argument in *Between Facts and Norms*.[8] He sets up a contrast between the classically liberal paradigm of private law and its subsequent social-welfare transformation. The first operated as if individual self-determination were adequately guaranteed by a certain set of (what we could call 'formal') rights. The second insisted on the 'factual' conditions for the exercise of autonomy, and the welfare entitlements necessary to secure it. But the social-welfare paradigm, in Habermas's view, falls foul of the problem of paternalism, and this becomes particularly evident in what he calls the 'postmetaphysical conditions'[9] that provide us with no reference point for legitimacy beyond what emerges from 'the discursive opinion- and will-formation of equally enfranchised citizens'. The social-welfare paradigm presumes that it (they, somebody) already knows what we need for freedom and equality, and then sets about establishing the necessary forms of social intervention to meet these requirements. Both the liberal and the social-welfare paradigm 'lose sight of the internal relation between private and *political* autonomy, and thus lose sight of the democratic meaning of the community's self-organization'.[10]

For Habermas, as for Young, there have to be procedures of political inclusion that will enable all those affected by decisions to engage in the political debate. 'Rights can be "enjoyed" only insofar as one *exercises* them.'[11] Or more specifically: 'Rights can empower women to shape their own lives autonomously only to the extent that these rights also facilitate equal participation in the practice of civic self-determination, because only women themselves can clarify the "relevant aspects" that define equality and inequality for a given matter.'[12] The argument is partly that the most well-intentioned paternalism will still get things wrong (there being no reason to believe you have got things right unless all possibly affected persons have had the chance to participate in and contribute to the discussion), and partly that the normative key is autonomy rather than well-being. Politics then becomes all-important – which for both Young and Habermas means politics in a broader sense than just participating in elections.

In my own work on political representation[13] I have focused more narrowly on the equitable representation of women and people from ethnic and racial minorities in decision-making bodies, and argued for affirmative action to secure fair representation. This shifts attention from transformations in the sexual or social division of labour to what its critics regard as 'political fixes': in recent European politics, the use of gender quotas to raise the number of women selected as parliamentary candidates; in post-1965 American politics, the creation of voting districts in which racial minorities form the voting majority and can secure the election of representatives from their own group. In both cases, the existing under-representation is self-evidently linked to patterns of social and economic inequality. If one wants to explain why so few women, for example, end up as political representatives, it is obvious enough that their positioning in the sexual division of labour is the major culprit. As long as women continue to shoulder the main responsibility for caring for the young, sick and old, it will be harder for women than men to envisage a full-time career in politics and less likely that they will present themselves as candidates for political office. We do not have to fall back on anything peculiar to female psychology, or demonstrate an age-old male conspiracy to hold on to political power; all we need is the banal observation that women look after children more often than do men. If this is what accounts for women's under-representation, critics may say, then the obsession with gender quotas is just another bad case of putting the cart before the horse: far better to concentrate on more nurseries, shorter working hours for parliamentarians, or getting the men to do their equal share. The problem with this is that it fails to consider seriously enough the conditions under which policies change. Calling for new policies without ever asking what would get these in place, it leaves the old cycle to continue as before.

Base–superstructure models convey a message of political despair, for why should one anticipate policies devoted to either sexual or racial equality from representatives who are almost exclusively white and male? How, indeed, are such representatives to know what policies are most appropriate if programmes for action are being worked out with minimal input from politically excluded groups? However causally correct the analysis that says women have been excluded from political activity because of the responsibilities they shoulder for care, it is inconceivable that a legislature composed primarily of men would undertake the necessary upheavals to alter this structural imbalance. What, in their knowledge or experience, would drive them to regard this as such a priority? Of course political inequalities reflect patterns of social and economic inequality: if overt discrimination has been banned and its incidence is reasonably well policed, any remaining differences in levels of participation or representation must arise from something in the structures of social life. (The only other explanation is that the differences are genetic, but I leave that to the geneticists to prove.) The big question is how to alter this pattern – and changing the people who formulate the policies looks a promising start.

Even when inequalities are grounded in social and economic conditions, there is then a strong case for political intervention. There is also, to bring in the second argument, more room for manoeuvre on the political than the economic terrain. Contemporary culture has become astonishingly fatalistic about economic inequalities, regarding them either as undesirable but inevitable, or even as positively fair. Political inequality, by contrast, is regarded as at odds with the principles of modern democracy. Despite its late and much contested arrival, political equality has established itself as part of the common sense of contemporary societies, achieving an almost foundational status. Confronted with evidence of political inequality or political exclusion, people are more likely to register this as an immediate and disturbing problem than when confronted with evidence of economic and social inequality. The interest in political equalization as a means of remedying or compensating for economic inequalities is partly a reflection of this.

Liberal critiques

One criticism of the above arguments is that they encourage a 'groupiness' that is at odds with individualism. Another is that the obsession with difference turns people in on themselves and away from ideas of a common good. We can agree, perhaps, that in a well-functioning democracy every (adult) member of the society would be equally included in the processes of political deliberation, and that there would be no category of people (women, blacks, the poor) left out. The key addition proposed in recent theories of democracy is that this equality will be arrived at only when currently marginal groups have been explicitly incorporated into the body politic. It is not good enough to say that there are no barriers to their inclusion, for if there are no barriers, how is it that members of these groups are so absent from the scene? Nor is it good enough to bring them in on condition that they leave their own group preoccupations behind, for if women are not permitted to speak from the experiences and perspectives of women, or black people from the experiences and perspectives of those who are black, who on earth is going to address their experiences and concerns? The point repeatedly made by critics is that this gives the impression that individuals are entirely defined by their sexual or racial or religious identities. Most people, they point out, do not define themselves narrowly by some group characteristic; and those who do should surely be encouraged out of exclusive identities rather than left mired in their own limited affairs.[14]

The idea that democracies might be expected to employ public resources to support and sustain minority cultural identities has proved particularly controversial, as has the related idea that they might exempt certain groups from legislation that otherwise applies to all. In both these cases, the main objection is that group characteristics or identities are being privileged over individual rights: either that individuals are being deprived of important and legitimate life-choices because of some supposedly over-riding community concern; or that certain individuals are being excused from obligations that will continue to bear on people elsewhere. The standard example of the first is the language legislation adopted by the Parti Québécois in 1977, which set strict limits to the public provision of English-language education and required commercial signage to be exclusively in French. Individuals who had previously been guaranteed the right to choose either French- or English-language schools for their children now had to rely on education in French, and the rights of the individual were then restricted in order to sustain the vitality of French language and culture. Examples of the second include legal exemptions granted to members of minority religious groups (like the exemption of Sikhs from legislation that requires motor-cycle riders to wear a crash helmet) that allow something to members of minority groups that is not permitted to the majority. In this case, group membership seems to carry with it certain favours: you get more freedom of movement by belonging to a particular minority than by belonging to the majority group.

This last complaint is, in my view, particularly misguided. Where such exemptions have been agreed, they are normally defended as necessary to enable members of minority groups to enjoy the *same* rights as the majority: in the above example, not to be prevented from riding motor-bikes because their cultural/religious conventions require them (but not other aspiring bikers) to wear a turban. The objective is not to give members of minority groups some extra rights or freedoms not enjoyed by the majority, but simply to enable them to have the same as their peers. This formulation is, in fact, a fairer description of all initiatives that could be said to provide extra rights or facilities to a particular sub-group of citizens, including cases where governments agree to provide additional resources to sustain a minority language or culture. When a group (or region or province) lays claims to a different schedule of rights or resources, it is always because it regards this as necessary to guarantee its equality with the others. When women, for example, campaign for special provisions to ensure the selection of more women as parliamentary candidates, they are not saying they want something more than is available to the men. They are saying that without those special provisions, they have no hope of getting the same. Or when Iris Young argues for special representation rights for members of oppressed groups (and not for others), she is not saying that people with a past experience of oppression should be compensated for their years of unhappiness by the chance to get more than the rest. She is saying that, without those special representation rights, oppressed groups have no hope of approaching an equality of influence.

A great deal of nonsense is talked about differential rights, as if these fundamentally subverted the very egalitarianism that has inspired them. There *are* difficulties, but these are largely to do with application rather than basic principle. Commenting on the criticisms of Quebec's language laws, Charles Taylor has said that 'there is a dangerous overlooking of an essential boundary in speaking of fundamental rights to things like commercial signage in the language of one's choice'.[15] Though I would probably disagree with Taylor on where to place the boundary, the general point seems right to me. I cannot get terribly agitated about the affront to individual freedom that comes from being obliged to read notices in French, though I do think that a country that is officially bilingual should provide children with access to schools in either language. (I also cannot get terribly agitated about the affront to individual freedom that comes with being denied access to a place of work when all the unionized employees are on strike, though I do think that a democratic society should allow people to choose whether or not to join unions.) Some things matter more than others, and refusing to consider (on principle) *any* curtailment of individual rights or *any* modification of equal treatment ignores what may be important differences of weight. A policy that curtails individual freedoms in order to promote collective concerns may or may not be defensible. We can hardly know which it is without establishing how important the particular freedoms and how shared the collective concerns.

Consider the argument that a ban on clitoridectomy appeals to the values of one cultural group to regulate the traditions of another, and that this imposition of liberal values on non-liberal cultures is inegalitarian and culturally imperialist. The problems with this argument include the following: (1) that the physical and emotional harm done to girls whose culture supposedly 'requires' their genital mutilation is severe, not trivial; (2) that as minors in a patriarchal culture, girls are in no position to indicate whether this practice really is important to their own sense of themselves; (3) that what are being presented as the shared values of a particular culture are, in this case, the values of its men. Compare this with the argument that requiring all motor-cyclists to wear a protective helmet sets considerations of health and safety above considerations of religion and culture, and indirectly discriminates against those whose culture requires them to wear a turban. I can imagine circumstances in which I would be equally dismissive of the second argument: I might not have much time for it if the mortality figures for those without helmets rose to 100 per cent, or if it turned out that the majority of Sikh men no longer bothered to wear turbans; I might then say Sikhs must choose between riding bikes and wearing their turbans. If (as it happens) I find the second argument perfectly acceptable, this is not because I have adopted a principled position about equity between cultural groups always trumping other considerations – any more than my objection to the first argument was premised on a principled position that differential treatment is always at odds with equality. In both cases, one needs to know something of the circumstances in order to judge. Since knowing something of the circumstances depends on who gets to speak and influence decision-making processes, this brings us back to the conditions for political inclusion.

The other criticism often levelled against the politics of difference is that the importance attached to representing 'group' concerns or perspectives can exaggerate the role of ascribed characteristics in the formation of political identities, and encourage a sedimentation of group differences that are better understood as fluid and shifting. It is one thing to say that democracies ought to be able to deal with women as women, not just as abstract citizens or surrogate men. It is still the case that women are not 'merely' women, but have formed their values, priorities and objectives out of unique combinations of experience that make each woman different from everyone else. (Nor are they 'merely' middle-class heterosexual white women, for adding in more precise specifications of the sub-group still exaggerates the role of ascribed characteristics.) Important as it is to challenge the false homogeneity that represses or denies group difference, it must be equally important to challenge the pressures of the group on the individual, and the way these can force people into a straitjacket of 'Irishness' or 'blackness' or 'femaleness' that represses differences between individuals. Many now talk of identities as hybrid, and see this as making a nonsense of simpler notions about 'black identity' or 'Asian identity' or 'female identity'. Even apart from these considerations, it is hard to see why defining oneself exclusively through one's group should be regarded as such a great achievement.

As applied to particular theorists, the criticism is largely misplaced, for most of those writing in this vein have been careful to distance themselves from 'essentialist' notions of what constitutes a group.[16] If, moreover, the critique is meant to imply that we should ignore evidence of group exclusion because the proposed remedies are worse than the disease, this hardly strikes me as an adequate response. There is still an important issue here. Nancy Fraser makes the point that much of the politics associated with women or racial minorities has been about putting 'gender' or 'race' out of business altogether – ending the feminization or racialization of the economy and abolishing those distinctions that place women or black people in the ranks of the over-exploited or under-paid. Claims for equality of recognition seem, however, to have the opposite effect. If the arguments developed in this chapter are right, tackling the under-valuation and/or exclusion of women and members of racial minorities will sometimes require more rather than less group differentiation: more emphasis on what makes the group distinct and different; less willingness to subsume these distinctions in grand notions of humanity or 'man'. As Fraser points out, this sets up a tension within egalitarian politics, part of which looks towards the dissolution of difference while the other seems to want difference more fully acknowledged. So do egalitarians want more difference or less? On the face of it, they seem to want both.

The main point I would make here is that there is a distinction between including/representing/revaluing 'a group' and including/representing/revaluing its members; it is the failure to make this distinction clearly enough that has generated much of the subsequent critique. Consider the example of political representation. Where subordinate groups can legitimately claim an under-representation in legislative chambers or decision-making bodies, the requirements of political equality suggest that 'their' level of representation should be raised. But who are 'they' in this case? If we mean the group *qua* group, this suggests a corporatist system of representation in which people will serve as representatives of their group, will be expected to speak on and for group issues, and will presumably be held accountable to members of that group. Such 'group' representation might be achieved through establishing separate electoral rolls for different groups (this is part of the mechanism for Maori representation in New Zealand); co-opting leading figures from the organizations that campaign on behalf of the group; or asking the group to generate its own representatives (through whatever mechanisms it chooses), who are then invited to join the decision-making body. As far as accountability is concerned, any of these looks reasonably promising, for all provide some mechanism through which members of the group can influence the policies pursued by their representatives. All of them, however, make the process of representation a specifically group affair. Representatives become spokespeople for group interests and perspectives; this is what they are there for, not any wider franchise.

The alternative is to say that the people marked by a particular group characteristic are under-represented (not then the group but those bearing group characteristics), and that we need to elect more representatives who share the markers and experiences of that group. It is this, rather than 'group' representation, that is being proposed in most of the current initiatives around raising the proportion of female or minority representatives: not a corporatist system of group representation that requires representatives to refer back to and speak for their group, but a more equitable distribution of representative positions between different social groups that brings a wider range of perspectives into play.

As compared with the first option, this offers very little in the way of accountability. If they are not elected by their group or linked in some formal way to group debates on priorities and policy, there is no obvious way of ensuring that Maoris will speak for the needs or concerns of Maoris, women for the needs or concerns of women, or African Americans for the needs and concerns of African Americans. There is no chain of accountability requiring these 'representatives' to follow group policies or concerns. The downside, then, is that people might be elected by virtue of their sex, ethnicity or race without this having much noticeable impact on the kinds of policy they decided to pursue. But while the second option is looser, less predictable, and less accountable, it is also less likely to lock people into narrowly bounded political identities. It does not treat people as if they are exclusively defined by group characteristics assigned to them or learnt, and it does not expect individuals to view everything from a narrowly 'group' point of view. The sense in which it is still about group representation is that it continues to recognize the crucial effects of group experience on political identities and aspirations, and insists on the importance of including people with different group experiences at the point where decisions are made. As a case for representation of the 'group', this would be vulnerable to criticism for exaggerating the power of ascribed characteristics or intensifying divisions between different groups. Understood as a case for raising the representation of group *members*, it is only vulnerable to criticism from those who think difference should not matter at all.

The hegemony of difference

Criticisms of the politics of difference are often based on misrepresentation and/or complacency, and while I see problems in many versions of identity politics, I do not regard the standard liberal reservations as decisive. The more serious difficulty, from my point of view, is that the hegemonic status of difference makes it hard to address inequalities that don't fit the picture. The shift from equality to difference does not indicate a lack of interest in equality, for discussions of sexual, racial, cultural, linguistic or ethnic difference are always framed by analysis of the

unequal power relations that have denied people full membership or recognition. And yet with the best of intentions, difference is not a category that can capture all relevant inequalities.
Nancy Fraser's question about whether the movements contesting gender or racial subordination are aiming at more or less difference is based on this point. Where social recognition is at
issue, it may be that groups need to assert and/or celebrate their
difference, for they need others to be willing to accept them as
equals while still accepting them for what they are. Where
equality in the labour force or housing market is at issue, assertions of difference may be just the opposite of what such groups
need.

Fraser's point is that 'difference' captures some but not all
injustices experienced by women or black minorities in a white-
dominated society, and that an exclusive emphasis on difference
will obscure some important inequalities. The further point is
that the hegemonic status of difference in contemporary social
and political thought can make it very difficult to talk about
class. Diana Coole argues that 'economic inequality is bracketed
out of discussion of difference',[17] which focuses by preference on
identity groups. We can of course talk about working-class
culture, but we cannot plausibly present the working class as a
cultural group fighting for recognition of its distinctive traditions
and culture. As Coole notes, celebrations of difference or 'open-
mindedness towards the Other' make little sense as applied to
class inequalities, for wherever people are positioned in the verti-
cal hierarchy of the capitalist economy, they will mostly agree
that it is better to be higher than lower. Currently dominant discourses of difference (whether these flow from feminism, post-
modernism, multiculturalism, or liberal traditions of tolerance
and respect) do not apply so readily to class as to gender, ethnicity
or culture. If all the problems of inequality are subsumed under a
general rubric of difference, this will leave class out in the cold.

In left politics, the hegemony of difference is illustrated by a
'radical pluralism' that always finds a place for class in its list of
oppressed or subordinated groups, but derives its categories of
analysis from the newer social movements that developed around
gender, sexuality or race.[18] In most discussions, class then seems
as much of an afterthought as 'women, blacks and gays' used to
be in socialist discourse of the 1960s and 1970s. In liberal theory,

the hegemony of difference is illustrated by the shift from questions of distributive justice to ones of cultural pluralism, a shift exemplified by the work of John Rawls. *A Theory of Justice*[19] generated a substantive thesis about the requirements of equality: the idea that inequalities in the distribution of primary goods were justified only when this distribution turned out to be of most benefit to the least advantaged. Rawls's later *Political Liberalism*[20] is almost exclusively preoccupied with the plurality of religious, philosophical, or moral doctrines that seem, on the face of it, to make it impossible to agree shared principles of justice. Liberalism has become increasingly troubled by accusations of cultural imperialism or the coercive imposition of liberal views: how to deal with difference then takes over from what kind of (economic) equality justice requires.

In this chapter, I have woven together what strike me as interrelated developments: the turn towards politics as something important in itself; and the reformulation of equality as depending on a recognition of difference. The two projects are not always connected. When David Marquand argues that the postwar emphasis on social rights encouraged a complacency about political and civil rights, making people think they already enjoyed their democratic equalities and only needed the jobs or hospital or schools, he can be taken as illustrating the renewal of politics. Marquand does not, however, reach this argument through an analysis of social pluralism, and has little to say about gender or racial difference. The connection between the two is not universal. Yet when put together, the combination has proved peculiarly inhospitable to economic concerns.

The implications of political equality are being stretched in much-needed directions, and I hope it is clear from what I have said that I welcome most of this development. Over the same period, analyses of economic equality have been pushed off into a separate realm, largely inhabited by theorists who have little sense of current debates about democracy or difference. This separation is itself symptomatic, and part of my aim in the next chapter is simply to bring some of that discussion of economic equality back into connection with democratic theory. The more specific objective is to consider whether economic equality matters in itself, before going on to discuss whether it should figure as a democratic condition.

3
Does Economic Equality Matter?

If, *per impossibile*, large economic inequalities did not threaten political, legal and social equality, they would be much less objectionable. But there might still be something wrong with them.[1]

The distribution of income and wealth poses problems for equal citizenship, but I leave these aside till the next chapter. The question here is whether economic equality can also be said to matter in itself. In pursuing this, I take it as given that it can matter without being the only thing that matters. Most discussions acknowledge further considerations that also have to be addressed; these usually include practical questions about keeping an economy running as well as principled issues about other values we hold equally dear. We might believe, for example, that it is inequitable to pay doctors more than nurses and that any well-regulated society would value each of these equally. (We might even think that doctors should be paid less than nurses, if we think they get more job satisfaction.) But we might still think that, failing the lure of a future high salary, no one would be daft enough to embark on the extra years of study necessary to qualify as a doctor. In a world regulated by market prices and dominated by rational choosers, we may have to put up with the inequality. We might believe it inequitable for those lucky enough to make a success of their business to end up with a fine mansion and several cars while those who fail through no fault of their own end up in bankruptcy proceedings. But if the mansion and cars turn out to be the only inducement that will encourage people to set up new enterprises, we may still think this a price worth paying.[2] We might believe that people should both start out and end up as economic equals, but if the only way to ensure this is through policing people's activities in every stage of their lives, we may find this an unacceptable level of state intervention. Michael Walzer sees the pursuit of literal equality as promoting 'a leveled and conformist society'.[3] Given the importance contemporary societies attach to autonomy and diversity, we may be unwilling to sacrifice these qualities even if we accept the independent value of economic equality.

To say that economic equality matters is not to say it is all that matters, for there may be further objectives that are threatened by the single-minded obsession with equality, and it is often necessary to modify the pursuit of one goal in order to address others equally pressing. But the main impression one gets from contemporary pronouncements is that the goal is not even important. The consensus, if any, is that 'literal', 'simple', 'levelling' equality is incoherent and deeply unattractive. 'Equality literally understood is an ideal ripe for betrayal',[4] and it is one we should do better without. This echoes Joseph Schumpeter's attack on the classical model of democracy (the idea that the pursuit of democracy is muddled by anachronistic attachment to ideals long past their relevance), but where principles of political equality seem to have survived relatively unscathed from the revisionist onslaught, there has been no such escape for economic equality. Indeed, the notion that equality means eliminating *all* inequalities in income or wealth has come to be regarded as so absurd that people are hard put to it to believe that anyone ever intended their equality so literally. 'Few people', we are told by the Commission on Social Justice, 'believe in arithmetical equality.'[5] 'Arithmetical' often signifies an unhealthy obsession with numbers; this is enough to make simpler egalitarians blush with shame.

Simple equality

The one exception usually allowed is Gracchus Babeuf, who attacked the French Revolution for betraying its own egalitarian principles and was executed for his role in the Conspiracy of the

Equals in 1797. Babeuf undoubtedly believed in a simple equality of wages, rejecting the 'plea of superior ability and industry' as 'an empty rationalization to mask the machinations of those who conspire against human equality and happiness'.[6] His take on this was, indeed, unique, for where subsequent egalitarians have usually welcomed superior ability or industry but queried whether these entitled people to extra rewards, Babeuf was more inclined to prevent the 'superior' individuals from making full use of their talents. 'Even a man who shows that he can do the work of four, and who consequently demands the wages of four, will still be an enemy of the people'; such a person 'should be allowed to perform no more than one man's work and to lay claim to no more than one man's pay'.[7] If the implementation of this strict egalitarianism meant that certain activities would no longer flourish, then so be it. 'Let the arts perish, if need be! But let us have real equality.'[8] For critics of simple equality, this declaration speaks for itself. Outside the excesses of the French Revolution, surely no one ever intended a strict equality in all income and wealth?

Rewriting history to eliminate what are now considered errors is a common human failing: rather than admitting to changing our minds, we often prefer to say our earlier opinions were misrepresented. Current takes on equality seem to me to fall into this pattern, but the idea that Babeuf was alone in taking his equality so literally does contain one element of truth. Egalitarians have tended to divide into those who saw the abolition of private property as the only way to secure full equality (this was a major part of Babeuf's argument), and those who accepted the framework of a market society as setting certain limits to the equality that could be achieved. The former were by far the more radical, anticipating a fundamental upheaval in social relations brought about by popular revolution, but the more they followed through their critique of the capitalist economy, the less willing they became to define their objectives just in terms of an egalitarian ideal. The latter took equality as a more central organizing principle, but because they accepted the framework of market relations and (to their credit) the requirement for majoritarian support, they tended to tailor their proposals to what they deemed politically and economically feasible. The former moved away from the simpler language of equality, while the latter accepted at least some of the case for monetary incentives. Neither then argued for that stricter equality of income that was so important to the Conspiracy of the Equals.

Marxists, in the first camp, rarely focused on inequality *per se*. Their organizing concepts were alienation, exploitation, oppression, and it was the power relations that subjected one class to another (and ultimately all classes to the juggernaut power of 'capital') that provided the main focus of their analysis. Marx famously criticized those of his contemporaries who took socialism to mean equal wages or a fair distribution, arguing that equality was a profoundly limited objective, appropriate perhaps to the first stage of socialism, but hardly to be promoted as a communist ideal. From a Marxist perspective, distribution is always secondary to production. Attempts to ensure an equitable distribution of labour or income or wealth were necessarily doomed unless the more fundamental relations of capitalist production – including the organization of producers into wage-labourers and the organization of production into the production of commodities for sale – were themselves transformed. It was impossible, in Marx's view, to eliminate inequality without first abolishing class society. But with the abolition of class society, it would become possible to go beyond the niggling exactitudes of equality into a deeper realm of freedom where each would give according to his (let us now add her) abilities and each receive according to his or her needs. Once labour had become 'not only a means of life but life's prime want',[9] we would no longer be constrained by questions of incentives or whether one person was getting as much as another. Equality, for Marx, was the protection people adopted in relations of deep inequality. Outside those relations, equality would be exposed as a limited ideal.

The catch, of course, was that the chances of achieving this depended on a degree of social (not to mention psychological) transformation that others have found historically implausible; and those less convinced by the fantasies of revolution have found it harder to credit this utopia beyond equality. Non-Marxist socialists presumed that societies would continue to be organized on the basis of wage labour and commodity production, and their conception of equality was then inevitably compromised by what they perceived as the necessities of market production. Even under conditions of greater equality, society would still face the question of incentives, for what would happen to economic creativity if no one could anticipate any additional rewards for risk-taking, imagination, or hard work? What, indeed, would happen to economic efficiency if the state took over the organization of all production, in the corner shops as well as the mines? Something, it was felt, would have to be left to private enterprise. If so, inequalities would inevitably develop between those who succeeded and those who failed. Where Marxists often dreamt of a withering away of the state, non-Marxist socialists tended to look to the state as the main engine of production and guarantee of equality, but most of them then recognized limits to what this state should do. Socialists were never as dismissive of individual liberties as their critics have liked to suggest, and most recoiled from the level of state intervention that would prove necessary to impose strict or literal equality. For reasons of efficiency and liberty alike, no non-Marxist socialist believed that strict equality could ever be achieved.

One might then agree that there has never been a significant strand of critical thinking that took strict equality as its goal: economic equality was always just a staging post en route to a higher form of social organization, or something that would have to be moderated by other concerns. But even if we allow this, there is still a notable difference between these older arguments and the ones that are presented today. Earlier egalitarians recognized a necessity for compromise, but what they were compromising was arguably an ideal of simple equality. Many people who have believed any income differential to be unjustified have argued for a reduction in income differentials rather than their elimination, or supported an 80 per cent tax on inheritance rather than the 100 per cent that simple equality seems to imply. But for much of this century, egalitarians still held on to notions of simple equality. They recognized, perhaps, that this equality was not as simple as it looked, but they still regarded it as the measure against which to judge the improvements they favoured.

If we consider the unlikely character of John Rawls in this connection – unlikely only because Rawls is a liberal with a strong commitment to equality rather than a self-declared socialist – it is clear enough that his *Theory of Justice* relies on a principle of simple equality. 'All social primary goods – liberty and opportunity, income and wealth, and the bases of self-respect – are to be distributed equally.'[10] Rawls arrived at this through an extraordinarily radical attack on the notion of desert. We do not 'deserve', he argued, those goods that come to us by our chance location in the existing social hierarchy: the wealth we inherited from our parents; the educational advantages we derived from access to private schooling; the political influence we wield through knowing the right people and mixing in the right social class. But neither do we deserve those goods that come to us by virtue of our own 'natural' abilities: our greater capacity for intellectual labour; our unusual gift for dreaming up new inventions; our greater stamina or strength. These are, as we so often say, 'gifts'. They come to us through no intrinsic merit of our own but through our good fortune in the natural lottery. If we do not think that social contingencies justify a moral claim to more or better goods, why should we think natural contingencies justify one person having more than another? 'From a moral standpoint the two seem equally arbitrary.'[11]

As it happens, Rawls immediately moderated his principle of simple equality, going on to say that all social primary goods 'are to be distributed equally *unless* [my emphasis] an unequal distribution of any or all of these goods is to the advantage of the least favoured'.[12] The ideal can be compromised, though only within certain limits that include the equal opportunity for all to reach any office or position. But if this condition is met, and it can be additionally shown that social and economic inequalities have been arranged to the greatest benefit of the least advantaged, then the fact that no one 'deserves' more than anyone else is not a good enough reason to refuse them. If, for example, extreme income differentials and the accumulation of extraordinary personal wealth turn out to provide the most efficient way of increasing production, and the greater productivity raises the living standards of the poorest to a higher level than they would enjoy in a regime of simple equality, then these inequalities are justified.

The conclusion is not particularly egalitarian. There has to be some compensation for the less fortunate (otherwise why would they accept the unequal society as a legitimate state of affairs?), but critics have argued that Rawls's principles of justice could condone a society of great inequality. The point to note is that the structure of Rawls's argument fits into what I have suggested was a common pattern through much of the twentieth century. The ideal equality is a simple equality (what Dworkin, in his critique of Rawls, describes as a 'flat' equality),[13] and there is no moral reason for querying this ideal. It may take second place behind even more fundamental principles of liberty, and may get compromised for reasons to do with efficient production, but it remains a simple or literal ideal.

I would say that feminist ideals of equality are also best understood within a framework of literal or strict equality, in that they argue for no difference between the sexes in any social sphere. For many feminists, sexual equality has meant just that: it has meant men and women sharing equally in carework (not men doing 'a bit more' housework or taking 'a bit more' responsibility for their children); men and women being equally represented in all the occupations within the society; men and women being elected in equal numbers to all the decision-making arenas, including the legislative assembly. It might be said that those who propose this vision of literal sexual equality remain agnostic about the other inequalities in society. They leave open, that is, the question of whether nursery workers should earn the same as judges, and merely insist that men and women should be equally represented in both fields of employment. But even with this caveat in mind, this is still a version of sexual equality that refuses to credit any of the claims of differential ability or strength and recommends literal or 'strict' equality. From this perspective (one I still broadly share), there is no significant space to be inserted between equality of opportunity and equality of outcome when it comes to sexual or racial equality. If the outcomes turn out to be statistically related to sex, the opportunities were almost certainly unequal.

My first point, then, is that simple equality has had a longer and more active life than is sometimes suggested today, and even when compromised by what are seen as other important considerations, has continued to inform egalitarian thinking through much of the nineteenth and twentieth centuries. Yet when we turn to the dominant debates of the 1980s and 1990s, we find this kind of equality no longer valued even as an ideal. The ideal of strict sexual equality is pilloried as ignoring 'profound sexually based differences between mothers and fathers',[14] and is contested (by feminists and non-feminists alike) as injecting those niggling exactitudes of equality into arenas better regulated by love or generosity or care. In their pronouncements on economic equality, politicians increasingly treat equality of outcome as not only impossible but actively unfair: a denial of individual autonomy and responsibility that no fair-minded person could possibly support. Meanwhile, in the theoretical literature, 'money egalitarianism' has virtually gone. The majority of theorists say that inequalities are justified when they arise from individual ambition and choice; or that we should be ensuring people a sufficiency rather than worrying about whether they have equal amounts; or that money inequalities are irrelevant so long as money cannot purchase all the other good things in life. Some of these arguments come from self-identified egalitarians, who argue that the meaning of equality has been misrepresented in simple notions of money equality. Others explicitly query the value of equality and argue that we should address hunger or poverty instead. Whatever the position, the results seem to mark a retreat from economic equality.

The retreat from economic equality

One could say it was wrong to pay one man more than another because there should be distribution according to needs. One could say it was wrong to pay the lazy scientist more than the diligent dustman because there should be distribution according to effort. One could say it was wrong to pay the intelligent more than the stupid because society should compensate for genetic injustice. One could say it was wrong to pay the stupid more than the intelligent because society should compensate for the unhappiness which is the usual lot of the intelligent. (No one can do much about the brilliant, they will be miserable anyway.) . . . One could say it was wrong to pay people who liked their work as much as those who didn't. One could – and did – say anything, and whatever one said it was always with the support of the particular kind of justice invoked by principles implicit in the statement.[15]

This extract from Michael Young's *Rise of the Meritocracy* illustrates one of the problems already rehearsed in discussions of economic equality, for there seem to be endless ways of interpreting what counts as fair or equal treatment, and no easy answer to what economic equality means. I will not attempt to summarize the entire field of discussion, but two main arguments surface with particular regularity. The first is that equalizing social resources is a very hit-and-miss way of achieving equality, for it pays no attention to differences in needs or desires. This is a point made long ago by Karl Marx when he observed (from a typically masculine perspective) that a single worker needs less to live on than a married worker with dependent wife and children, and that giving each of these an equal income will not produce an equal effect. Later theorists have usually managed to avoid this uncritical invocation of the male breadwinner/female dependant, but they have reiterated Marx's point about the complex relationship between resources and needs, and added in further questions about the different perceptions of what makes life good.

Equalizing social resources fails to deal with any 'natural' inequalities we may start out with: the good or bad luck that makes some people stronger, more talented, perhaps just more contented than others, and can prove far more decisive in determining the quality of our lives than our initial share of social resources. Equalizing social resources also fails to address the different value people attach to resources: the fact that some people may care more about time for contemplation or leisure than about the goods they are enabled to enjoy. In a strict division of the world's resources, 'almost everyone would end up with a very inconvenient bundle, with lots of useless items, but too little of what is really desired'.[16] A third of a cow, as David Miller suggests, but no share of a beautiful landscape – is this really what equality implies?

If we care about equality, it is presumably because we think it will promote people's welfare, and making a fetish of equal division looks a poor way of achieving this goal. Amartya Sen makes the point that it is not goods as such that should concern us but what they *do* to human beings.[17] Some people may need more than others in order to achieve a similar level of well-being: the obvious and much repeated example being the person who is born with a physical disability and needs additional equipment, like a wheelchair, to reach the standards of mobility that others have taken for granted. Children who suffer from dyslexia need additional educational support in order to develop their reading and writing potential; while those who are being educated in a language different from the one they use at home may need extra language tuition in order to do as well as their peers.

None of these examples looks particularly devastating, and it might seem easy enough to modify the notion of equal resources (make it a sum, perhaps, of 'inner' and 'outer' resources) so as to address such self-evident differences in need. Once we start, however, to inject some notion of differential need into the account of equality, we rapidly lose the attractive simplicity of equalizing everyone's amount. Thus it seems obvious enough to me that children who have special difficulties with learning should get extra attention so as to develop their full potential, and I can regard this as a minor qualification to the equality of resources so as to compensate for their greater need. But what of the seemingly parallel argument that children who are specially gifted should get extra attention in order to develop *their* full potential? Do we say that children who are already privileged in their own 'inner' resources should get less than the others; that they should get the same as the average; or that they are entitled to a larger share of educational resources because they too have special needs? Once we recognize (as I think we must) the inadequacies of a strict division of the world's resources, we seem to be plunged into impossible conundrums about how to deal with differential need.

One way out of this is to move from equality of resources to equality of welfare; we can then treat resources as a means to what really matters, which is equality in our sense of well-being. This falls prey, however, to the second objection much discussed in the literature, which is that equalizing welfare is an incoherent objective because of the difficulties in establishing what well-being means. What makes people contented varies. Indeed people vary even in the value they place on contentment. If we try to operate with 'objective' standards of welfare, this will lead us to favour some people's definitions over others: we may specify that everyone needs a certain amount of space to live in, for example, but what if some people are happiest when they live in close proximity to others, while others are only happy when they enjoy a level of privacy that depends on more personal space? Refusing to acknowledge these differences in subjective evaluation makes a mockery of the very notion of welfare, for how can we say that people have been made equal in their sense of well-being when some are patently dissatisfied with their lot? Yet if we try to accommodate these differences, this also threatens to make a mockery of the egalitarian objective. We might then find ourselves saying that people who are used to living in large houses are entitled to a larger share of social resources than the rest, or that those who are only happy drinking fine claret are entitled to more than those who gaily drink water from the tap. And what do we do to use Amartya Sen's example, for the cripple who has a jolly disposition, or whose 'heart leaps up whenever he sees a rainbow in the sky'?[18] Does the fact that so little makes him happy absolve society from any responsibility for meeting what might be described as his 'objective' needs?

Something goes wrong, in other words, with either of the standard alternatives. If we focus on an equal distribution of economic resources (or an equal distribution of Rawls's primary goods), we end up ignoring important differences in people's capacities and values, and produce outcomes that are far from equal. If we focus instead on equalizing people's sense of well-being, we end up giving more to the constitutionally dissatisfied and less to the easily content: the outcome may then be 'equal', but the means of achieving it favour the more over the less demanding and this will offend most egalitarian sensitivities. The further point often made by people who are unhappy with the notion that we do not 'deserve' the fruits of our natural talents is that most of us seem willing to condone the high salaries paid to great singers or actors or athletes. We may object to the inflated salaries paid to company executives whose contribution to our well-being remains obscure, but we rarely mind when the activities have brought us real pleasure. These are the kinds of complication that are enough to turn you off equality for life. Some, at least, of the current retreat stems from the resulting sense of despair.

Opportunities and choice

Those who write on questions of equality have exhibited considerably more stamina, but there is a tendency to opt *either* for a refined version of equality of opportunity, *or* for a version of minimum conditions that turns away from equality to emphasize people's basic needs, *or* for a reduction in the power of money that leaves money inequalities still intact. The first of these is particularly compelling for those who want to leave space in their egalitarianism for the exercise of individual choice or the recognition of individual responsibility, and see this as incompatible with equality of outcome. Though he describes his position in terms of 'equality of resources', Ronald Dworkin falls into this first camp. Welfarism is unacceptable, he argues, because we have to have some way of excluding unreasonable requirements.[19] Faced with people who never feel satisfied with what they have achieved, or never feel happy with their lot, we have to be able to say that some regrets are unreasonable. And faced with people who have what he calls 'champagne tastes', we have to be able to say that there is a difference between a reasonable claim for sustenance and the unreasonable dependency on the finest of wines. In doing so, however, we fall back on an alternative notion of fair distribution that cannot be translated into welfare: some independent idea of what counts as a fair share of social resources, regardless of what it does to people's sense of well-being. This brings Dworkin round to a defence of equality of resources, but what he means by this has little to do with equality of outcome. Equality of resources does not mean equalizing 'the quantity of disposable goods or liquid assets people command at a particular time';[20] it requires, rather, 'that people pay the true cost of the lives that they lead'.[21]

The distribution of resources should not reflect the chance differences in ability that we are born with (this is the important sense in which Dworkin defends equality of resources), but it is entirely right and proper that it should reflect the different choices we make in our lives. The person who chooses to work is entitled to a higher income than the person who chooses not to; the person who saves for the future is entitled to a better retirement than the person who spends all income as it comes in; or, to use one of Dworkin's more unpleasant examples, the person who insures against blindness is entitled to compensation when the person who chose not to is not.[22] An obsession with after-the-event money equality discounts the choices people have made about what to do with their resources; it also discounts the very different attitudes people adopt towards money and wealth. (Once people are free of genuine poverty, Dworkin argues, there is no reason to think that everyone would want to be rich; the idea that the best life is the life dedicated to the accumulation of wealth or the consumption of luxuries 'comes as close as any theory of the good life to naked absurdity'.)[23] What we need is a way of distinguishing between those inequalities that arise out of natural disadvantage and those that legitimately reflect our tastes and choices; the first are rightly treated as inequalities, the second are better described as differences and not to be treated as evidence of injustice.

Translated into the more standard opposition between equality of opportunities and equality of outcome, this is clearly an argument that favours the former. It is, admittedly, a particularly radical version of equal opportunities, for it justifies only those inequalities that derive from differences in choice, and looks to taxation to redistribute those further advantages that derive from differences in natural talent.[24] It sees the chance endowments of beauty, intelligence, or strength as no more than chance endowments, and has little time for the conventional notion that talented people 'deserve' their greater rewards. In the framework of a market society, these chances will have their usual effect: Dworkin is not suggesting that everyone should earn the same, regardless of abilities or talents. His point, rather, is that those who earn more than the average should not regard the extra as something that is theirs by right. They have it because they were lucky and shouldn't grumble if some is taken away. The policy implications then end up close to those that emerge from Rawls's *Theory of Justice*: an unequal (market) society, qualified by progressive taxation, providing the basic elements of a welfare state. But where Rawls retains the presumption in favour of an equal distribution, Dworkin no longer has any time for simple or flat equality.[25] Such equality is not just practically unworkable, or less efficient in improving the quality of life. It is no longer to be defended even as an ideal.

Some of this will strike a resonant chord, for most of us probably do think that people should carry the consequences of (at least some of) their actions. We do not normally object when those who postpone their early chances of earning a decent income in order to get more qualifications later benefit from a higher salary; or when those who give up on exotic holidays in order to pay for their mortgage end up with better accommodation than their more frivolous friends. Those of us in public employment often feel our incomes falling unfairly behind those in the private sector, but we may still feel that people who took on the greater insecurities of the private sector (and even more so, those who took on the risks associated with running their own business) are entitled to the rewards of their choice if the gamble eventually pays off.

Note, however, that such examples present structures of inequality as arising from the discrete choices of autonomous individuals. The point about this is not just that it abstracts from the background constraints and opportunities that make it easier for some people to take risks than others: the fact that it is easier to risk extended periods of study, for example, if your family is prepared to support you; or that it may be impossible to contemplate taking out a mortgage unless you already have a certain amount in the bank. Most contemporary theorists of equality are well aware of these 'imperfections' – that is what they are attempting to deal with when they distinguish between the unfair effects of inherited inequalities and the legitimate consequences of individual choice. But even when this is the stated intention, the focus on individual comparisons still tends to anaesthetize people against what they know to be major differences in opportunities and power. In abstracting from social relations, they also abstract from dominance: the fact that one person's choice is so often enabled by another's lack of choices, or that one person's success may depend on exploiting other people.

The wealth of the household with two or more high earners, for example, is made possible not just by the individuals' choices and ambitions, but by the low wages they can pay to others: the cleaners, nannies, gardeners, etc. who free the members of that household to embark on their well-paid careers. To take this a generation back, the wealth of a high-earning man is made possible not just by his individual ambitions, but by the availability of a non-earning wife who frees him from housework and childcare. In both cases, the opportunities seized upon by the energetic and ambitious only exist because there are others who have no chance of doing the same, and it would be logically impossible for everyone to make the same choices. There is a deep structural inequality here, and it is even deeper than the one that propels children of working-class parents into working-class jobs and children of professional parents in the opposite direction. It is not just that some individuals have been more favoured than others by the circumstances they grew up in: given an earlier start in the race or allowed to use performance-enhancing drugs. In the examples given above, one person is being favoured precisely because another is less so: the good luck of one actually depends on the bad luck of the other.

To move the argument even more decisively from comparisons between individual choosers, the wealth of the private company still derives from the labour of its employees, and exploitation does not magically vanish just because individuals have some choice over what jobs they do. Yet this last element is curiously absent in current discussions of inequality. Ronald Dworkin has observed that notions of 'flat' equality become most obviously unsatisfactory when we try to apply them person by person, and that it is those theorists who persist in thinking of equality as a relationship between social groups who find themselves most drawn to ideals of simple equality.[26] For Dworkin, this is one of the reasons for switching our attention to the comparisons between individuals. But it is just as plausible to follow the argument to the opposite conclusion: to say that an unhealthy obsession with whether opera singer Maria is entitled to a higher income than surfer Bruce, or champagne drinker Charlie to a larger drinks budget than teetotaller Jane, obscures those structural inequalities that cannot be understood in such individualist terms.

This is a common failing in arguments that seek to justify those inequalities that arise from the exercise of personal choice, and it arises less from the importance attached to personal responsibility than from the amnesia about the relationship between social groups. If we are willing to accept that people are responsible for some of their actions – that people who commit a crime, for example, can be punished for what they do – it is indeed implausible to exempt those actions that have economic effects. Most of us will want to say that adults have a responsibility to care for their children at a vulnerable age. Saying this implies that adults can be criticized, in the worst cases punished, for failures in this field. What, then, is so different about having to accept the consequences of one's economic choices – and the conclusion that seems to follow from this, that some individuals will end up with more than others? The importance attached to personal responsibility does justify some of the inequalities in economic condition. The energy devoted to making this point has come, however, at the expense of sociological precision, leading to an exaggerated emphasis on individual comparisons and a corresponding lack of attention to relationships of dominance and power.

The other problem is that because the examples are designed to show us that some inequalities are justified, they take us away from sharper perceptions of what people need. We are drawn again and again into comparisons that direct us to two individuals who enjoy the same range of talents and opportunities, but choose to do different things with them: the person who chooses to play tennis all day versus the neighbour who plants a garden and ends up generating a higher income from the sale of her wonderful vegetables;[27] the person who chooses to work a full week versus the colleague who splits his week between part-time employment and the cultivation of his roses.[28] The idea is to get us to focus more precisely on what it is about inequality that bothers us, but the choice of comparisons also skews the conclusions in a particular way. When we compare individuals who are hypothetically placed with the same range of opportunities and prospects, any subsequent inequalities between them become more intuitively acceptable. But once we have accepted the justice of some inequalities, we may find it harder to get back to notions of what any individual needs.

Amartya Sen reminds us that 'giving more income to the naturally talented people does, of course, amount to giving less to those without talents', and when the latter include 'the old and the infirm stripped of their talents by the natural process of aging',[29] this casts a disturbing shadow over an exclusively merit-oriented system of desert. But giving more income to the naturally ambitious or naturally far-sighted also amounts to giving less to those who frittered away their time on roses and tennis. If these latter end up with an income below what is normally regarded as necessary to existence, we may still see the results as unacceptable.

Comparing individuals who are supposed to be similarly situated gets us into a rather punitive frame of mind, somewhat akin to those Victorian distinctions between the deserving and undeserving poor. But needs do not go away just because the needy made mistakes. Indeed, one might want to question whether anyone should be required to bear the consequences of her choices when these lead to a situation no sane person would deliberately pursue. (I am reminded here of those questions about whether a just God could condemn anyone to the everlasting torments of hell, or whether even the worst of sinners could legitimately plead ignorance and work out his redemption through purgatory.) Even if we want a version of equality that leaves space for individuals assuming responsibility for their lives, we cannot humanely pursue the notion of what people have 'chosen' or 'deserved' to the point of condemning them to destitution. If we want to stop short of this, it means that an initial equality of resources, combined with an equal opportunity to make what we choose of them, fails to satisfy the requirements of equality.

From equality to sufficiency

This is where the second alternative comes into play. Instead of reworking the notion of equality to distinguish between the illegitimate inequalities that arise from unfair advantages and the legitimate ones that arise from people's active choice, perhaps we should be focusing on what any human being needs in order to live a decent life? Questions of desert would be irrelevant here. All human beings, by virtue simply of their humanity, would be regarded as entitled to what is necessary to a decent quality of life, and the needs of the poorest would then take priority in the distribution of social resources. The emphasis on opportunities and choices encourages us to ignore those many members of the society who could not (or perhaps just did not) avail themselves of the opportunities. The alternative emphasis on meeting basic needs refuses to engage in metaphysical questions about whether people 'chose' their poverty, or failed through no fault of their own. However they got there, their needs still speak for themselves.

In societies that are all too willing to blame the poor for their poverty, this is an attractive alternative. The point made by a number of theorists is that it does not say anything about equality. Equality implies comparison – do I have more or less the same as you? – but the compulsion to eradicate poverty or meet basic human needs arises more from humanitarian impulse than anything to do with equality. In Harry Frankfurt's formulation, the sufficiency argument effectively drops the pursuit of equality: what matters 'is not that everyone should have the *same* but that each should have *enough*'.[30] So long as each of us has a sufficiency of resources – enough, that is, to satisfy any reasonable person and enable her to pursue her basic aims – then there may be no moral significance attached to whether other people enjoy far more. Indeed, Frankfurt argues that the obsession with comparison alienates us from ourselves, for instead of focusing on what we need to do the things we care about, we focus on other people and how much more they have.

This is an argument much loved by contemporary politicians who recurrently warn us against the 'politics of envy' – and there is an important point in this. Many will agree about the corrosiveness of envy and the way it can destroy what would otherwise be a perfectly satisfactory life; with this in mind, we might well want to say that we should drop the obsession with equality to focus on more immediate questions about eliminating poverty and hunger. Joseph Raz notes that we do not bother ourselves unduly about an unequal distribution of grains of sand, presumably because we do not see possession or otherwise of sand as mattering very much to our life. We do, by contrast, worry about one person being hungry when another is replete, but he suggests that it is not the inequality that bothers us in this so much as the fact that someone is hungry.[31] 'Rhetorical egalitarianism' adds nothing, in his view, to the humanistic concern with alleviating hunger. If we can address the hunger – and by extension, the much higher 'sufficiency' level that may be necessary to provide people with a decent quality of life – who cares if others are

enjoying much more? Equality forces us into continual comparisons with others, and because of that, it never seems able to
stop. From the basic needs or sufficiency perspective, comparative inequalities are inconsequential so long as human needs are
met.

In this argument, we are asked to step back from the obsession
with equality and consider what we want the equality for. If
the pursuit of equality is designed to eliminate the barbarism
that condemns some members of a community to malnutrition,
over-crowding, or hypothermia while other members of that
community rejoice in more material wealth than they could possibly use, then maybe the point of the comparison is simply that
there is enough wealth around to remedy the poverty. So let's
remedy the poverty, and not get sidetracked by inequality *per se.*
Money inequality no longer figures as the villain of the peace: it
becomes morally insignificant whether income differentials range
from 1:10 or 1:100, so long as no one is deprived of what is
necessary to life. What matters is sufficiency – which, in fairness
to the argument, may be set at a far more generous level than in
the standard measures of poverty.

I have some sympathy with this, for I do think that the images
of poverty in the midst of wealth are what give greatest urgency
to egalitarian politics, and that these images are far more compelling than the fact that some people drive Jaguars while others
make do with the cheapest of Fords. When we also worry about
the relative positioning of people on the total social scale, it is
often because of the implications that flow from this when it
comes to political equality. To that extent, it may be that economic inequality matters less for itself than in its relationship to
political equality. I return to this in the next chapter. At this
stage, I just want to register two problems with the sufficiency
argument.

The first is that what we regard as sufficient is itself condi-
tioned by what those richer than us enjoy. This is not only for
reasons of envy. In a society where access to the common culture
has come to depend on watching the same programmes on TV,
having a television set becomes a necessity rather than a luxury.
In a society where car ownership has become widespread, it can
be hard for those without cars to get access to basic amenities:
shopping centres are often located in areas difficult to reach by

public transport; indeed public transport may collapse when the richer members of the community no longer use it. Sen quotes Adam Smith on what one needs to appear in public without shame:[32] this is a comment that will speak volumes to those hard-pressed parents who have enough to buy shoes for their children but not enough for trainers in the requisite mode. The wealth and consumption patterns of the richer members of society set new standards for the poorer members, and while some of this could be discounted as the unhealthy reflection of a materialistic society, much of it enters into what one 'needs' to take part in the life of the community. This suggests that sufficiency levels vary with the degree of inequality; that what is sufficient to the quality of life in a more egalitarian society may not be sufficient in a less egalitarian one. If so, then sufficiency is not logically distinct from equality.

The second point is that if inequalities in income and wealth cannot be justified (other than by the fact that they are there), then it seems odd to say we should not allow them to bother us. We might agree that the urgent issue is whether everyone in society has enough, and that addressing the condition of those worst off should be the priority for any egalitarian politics. If we continue to think, however, that the rich got where they are by their ancestors' robbery and pillage, that people working in 'male' fields of employment are deriving inflated salaries from the historical under-valuation of female labour, or that company executives are paying themselves illegitimate rewards just because they have the power to do so, then the knowledge that everyone else now has enough will hardly satisfy us. Egalitarianism may not require a total equality in money incomes, and the issues raised over what it means to equalize either resources or welfare indicate some of the difficulties with such an approach. There is still a question about which inequalities, if any, can be justified, and those that derive from an abuse of power seem self-evidently unfair.

In line with Rawls and Dworkin, I see any inequalities that derive from natural differences in talent as unfair, but am willing to limit my critique to those that can be shown to rise from historical accident: the kind of historical 'accident' that has over-valued male jobs in comparison to female ones, mental labour in comparison to manual, or work in the financial sector over work in other kinds of service. To take one telling example, jobs categorized as 'women's work' tend to be more poorly paid than those categorized as men's even where the skills required to carry out the former are greater; and when previously male jobs become feminized (as was the case with medicine in the former Soviet Union), the wage attached to them typically drops. Income differentials do not reflect straightforward differences in the nature of the work: how difficult it is, or how rare the talents it requires. Far more commonly, they reflect historical patterns that have allocated certain kinds of work to the public sector and others to the private sector, or have valued the work of some groups of workers less highly than the work of others. Even if the market were a fair way of allocating rewards (and it is hard to see why it should be, given that market prices reflect what is already an inequality in purchasing power), certain groups of workers have always engaged in rent-seeking activities that push up their own rewards. It has been standard practice in many professions to restrict entry so as to maintain high incomes; standard practice, also, in skilled manual work, where apprenticeship schemes not only provided the necessary training but kept the number of entrants down. If we take income differentials as they are, in their often patent absurdity, it becomes impossible to question the justice of the existing order. Yet this is precisely what the sufficiency argument seems to suggest: stop bothering your head about inequalities in income or wealth and get on with tackling the poverty. It is hard to see how this could be thought fair.

From simple to complex equality

There is a third line of argument that discourages us from focusing on money inequalities, most powerfully developed by Michael Walzer in his case for 'complex equality'.[33] Walzer also claims that money inequalities are inconsequential, or rather that if they can be shorn of their usual consequences, then the requirements of equality will be met. In contrast to most of today's writers on equality, Walzer puts notions of dominance and subordination at the centre of his analysis. He does so, however, only to reiterate the point that economic equality is not the main concern. Simple egalitarians, he argues, are obsessed with monopolies, with the fact that one group of people has monopolized what should in justice be shared out. Complex egalitarians focus instead on dominance, on the way that access to one social good has given people the power (or made them believe they have the right) to claim another. When those who have excelled in the making of money, for example, employ this to purchase wives, qualifications, or political influence, they are invading the separate spheres of love or education or politics. They are trying to employ what may be quite legitimately theirs in the sphere of the market to exert an illegitimate dominance elsewhere.

Walzer argues that each sphere has its own internal principles of fair distribution, and that instead of trying to suppress what we see as the inequalities of money, we should concentrate on putting it in its place. (We should also, of course, work to keep love or education in their place, for while it is entirely appropriate that we should favour those we love when deciding who to spend the rest of our lives with, it will not be appropriate to favour them in deciding who gets which job; and while it may be entirely appropriate to favour the smartest in allocating university places, it will not be appropriate to favour them in deciding who is excused from military service.)

The intuitive attractiveness of this lies in the commonsense perception that those who are good at one thing are not necessarily so good at everything else: that one person may be good at making money, another at playing football, another at passing exams. A society that values only one of these qualities, or allows those who excel in one to grab all the honours in everything else, strikes us as particularly inequitable. This is the key point made in Michael Young's critique of the meritocratic society: that a society which uses intelligence tests to allocate occupations, status, income and political power undermines all alternative sources of self-respect and ends up destroying the basis for human equality. Measuring people along a single axis – whether this be birth or wealth or intelligence – divides people inexorably into the haves and have-nots. But it may not be the inequalities that matter so much as whether those inequalities have become general.

Like the sufficiency argument, this asks us to stand back from the obsession with money inequality and consider what it is about inequality that bothers us. If it is the stark division of society into the haves and have-nots, then maybe the point of the comparison is not that some have more than others but that some have more than others in every single sphere. So let's tackle the accumulation of inequalities, and not get sidetracked by inequality wherever it appears. Who cares about the money so long as each has a chance of success in one of society's other spheres?

One problem is that this seems to assume that virtually any distribution of money inequalities is fair; like the sufficiency argument, it then draws attention away from inequities in the pattern of income differentials, giving the impression that any distribution is just. The key objection raised against the sufficiency argument would then apply equally here. A second problem is that even if we did keep money more firmly in its place, there would still be a chance of general inequality. Some people might just turn out to excel in every sphere of social existence, and might quite legitimately end up with the most love, the best health, the highest qualifications and the most money. Others might be good at nothing and end up with nothing at all. Walzer is clearly not happy with such a scenario. He notes that if a society characterized by complex equality ended up favouring the same individuals every time, 'this would certainly make for an inegalitarian society',[34] and this comment has suggested to some critics that more old-fashioned ideals of literal equality still linger in the background of his thought.[35]

The more correct reading, in my view, lies in Walzer's own statement of his aims as a society free from domination, the point being not to ensure an equal distribution of resources, but to eliminate the experience of personal subordination. 'This is the lively hope named by the word *equality*: no more bowing and scraping, fawning and toadying; no more fearful trembling; no more high-and-mightiness; no more masters, no more slaves.'[36] Such a hope would clearly be threatened by an accumulation of successes on one side and failures on another, but Walzer argues that where this happens, we should take it as evidence that domination still remains. His belief that money inequality need not spell general inequality is partly founded on what he describes as a 'democratic wager':[37] the belief that qualities and talents are roughly distributed across the population, so that those who do badly in one sphere of life will be compensated by success in another sphere. Can we really imagine that the qualities that make people restless risk-takers, caring parents, precise perfectionists, skilful orators, wise friends will be found in a single person? Is it not far more plausible to think that the diversity of intelligences and talents is so distributed that everyone has something and no one comes near to having the lot? I agree with Walzer on this. I also agree with the conclusion he draws from it, that when people end up failing in every sphere of life, we should assume that their society is failing them rather than that they are 'natural' failures.

But when Walzer talks of a society in which inequalities no longer matter because the inequalities are not general, I still doubt his sociology. The third – most damning – difficulty is just that money has such exorbitant power. Knowing what we do of market society, it is hard to envisage a really consistent containment of the powers of money: indeed Walzer himself notes that 'short of separating children from their parents', it would be difficult to prevent the rich from turning their money to the educational advantage of their children.[38] Even if we abolished private health care and private education, money would still buy better health, a longer life, better education, for one can hardly say that people are entitled to their money but then prevent them using it to buy better food, more holidays or more books. (The whole point about money is that it is so infinitely convertible.) And even with a really rigorous policing of the boundaries, money would still carry authority, for one of the defining characteristics of a market society is that it employs wealth as a measure of power.

Money, as we know, is not supposed to buy political favours, but one can hardly ignore the extraordinary political influence of the media barons or the greater authority of the wealthy in deciding between policy alternatives. Writing in the American context, Walzer has argued for constraints on campaign finance that would moderate the power of money in American politics. But even if people were prepared to set a limit to party donations – or more radically, to fund party activities from the public purse – money would continue to exert its disproportionate influence. It would still skew access to political office to favour the more privileged members of the society; and would still lend additional weight to the opinions of those who have proved themselves successes in the economic field. The British Parliament does not attract the richest members of the society, but there continues to be a significant over-representation of that 7 per cent of the population who are educated in private schools. And regardless, it seems, of the political complexion of the party in power, the big names in industry or commerce or finance still carry disproportionate authority when it comes to advising on which policies to pursue. In the framework of a market society, money is both access and authority. This is one of the reasons egalitarians worry so much about its distribution.

Does economic equality matter?

This, of course, is Walzer's point (if money no longer provided access or authority, perhaps we could stop worrying about its distribution), and one of the strengths of his analysis is that it helps focus on why the distribution of economic resources might be regarded as such a pressing concern. My answer so far has followed a reasonably well-worn path. I criticize merit where there is no deserving (you cannot be said to 'deserve' higher payment for something that is a function of privilege or just the luck of the draw), but say that where there *is* a genuine choice, people should accept some of the consequences of their actions. (Only some, for a humane society will always ensure that citizens are provided with the minimum necessary for life.) Since individuals do have some choices about and responsibility for their economic actions, this means I do not defend strict equality of outcome. A humane society would ensure that everyone has enough resources to maintain a decent standard of life; beyond that requirement, it could not regard inequalities that derive from the exercise of individual choice as illegitimate. The key point is still that individuals have nothing like complete choice over their actions, and this entails deep scepticism about existing differentials in income or wealth.

Inequalities that derive from the privileging of particular groups of people and/or particular types of work are unjust and should be eliminated. This is a pretty large category. It includes cases where people are being penalized for the good or bad luck of being born female rather than male, black rather than white, or with a serious physical disability. More contentiously but still pretty plausibly, it includes cases where people are being penalized for the family circumstances they happened to be born into, the chances that delivered them to parents who are poor rather than rich, or to a neighbourhood that lacks decent schools. It also includes what, in my view, is the large number of cases where the social valuation accorded to capabilities and talents has been marked by historical distortion, reflecting the unfair privileging of certain kinds of labour or the rent-seeking activities of certain social groups. The first two imply a strong version of equal opportunities: serious and sustained initiatives (which might then include affirmative action) against racial, sexual, and other forms of discrimination; serious and sustained initiatives (which must surely mean more than the provision of publicly funded schools) against the privileges of inherited wealth. The third introduces something that has figured less prominently in recent discussions but will be familiar enough territory to anyone who has considered the differential rewards associated with 'men's' and 'women's' labour and the illegitimate privileging of one sex over another that so often goes with this. (It will also be familiar enough to anyone who has noticed and queried recent increases in top executive pay.) Discussions of equality often proceed as if the only choice is between equalizing people's chances to move into different slots, or else equalizing the rewards attached to each slot. There is an important third element, for even if we allow the legitimacy of differential rewards for differential work, the valuation currently attached to particular jobs is often highly questionable.

A society that remedied these inequalities would be in marked contrast to what most of us live in today, but might still be described as remedying distortions: those inequalities that arise from the exercise of 'illegitimate' privilege or 'unfair' discrimination. To push this an important step further, we should also be sceptical of income differentials when they arise from undistorted market relations. The conventional defence of market prices is that people are paid according to laws of supply and demand. If certain categories of work can only be done by graduates, and there is an under-supply of people with degrees, then 'of course' graduates will be paid more than the unskilled labourers who are chasing too few jobs. It is important to recognize this argument for what it is: an evacuation from the terrain of justice onto the terrain of what makes market sense. Unless we have independent reasons for believing markets to be moral (I can't myself see what these reasons might be), then the fact that an undistorted operation of the market would still generate differentials between one kind of job and another tells us nothing about what is fair. It only tells us what is 'natural' under market conditions, what happens unless we choose to moderate it. What the market delivers is not necessarily just: this is the crucial underpinning for any redistributive politics.

The final point (derived from Rawls rather than Marx) is that even if we could create an economy in which rewards 'fairly' reflected the inherent value of the work and individuals were 'genuinely' provided with an equal chance to try for the best jobs, the differential rewards attached to differential talents would still be unfair. The chance distribution of gifts and talents does not justify economic inequality. From a moral point of view, the natural contingencies of what we are born with are just as arbitrary as the social circumstances of our family or neighbourhood or nation.

I think Rawls is right on this, and that people should not be penalized just because they are born without the abilities most valued in their society. But what are the implications? Rawls decided not to pursue them too far, believing that any society that refused to reward the more talented would be condemning all its members to a reduced standard of living. What cannot be justified by intrinsic merit may then be justified by efficiency: no one with half a pretension to living in the real world could afford to ignore this point. The argument raises, however, a question about what it means to describe something as unfair. If we can say it is unfair (in one sense) and yet legitimate (in another) for those born with certain kinds of ability to be paid more than the rest, it seems that the critique of merit takes us less far than we might have expected. It begins to look more like an enabling argument, something that undermines what has been one of the main props for income differentials and clears the ground for a more rigorous equality. Whether any society acts on it will depend on the judgements its citizens make about efficiency. It will also, I think, depend on the judgements they make about the many things that make them unhappy.

Egalitarians do not (cannot) think that people have to be made equal in every respect. Genetic differences alone would make this unattainable, and once we add in the tragic chances of human existence (some people die young while others go mad), strict equality hardly seems a viable project. Indeed, the more we focus on what makes one life better than another, the less likely it is that we will come up with economic equality as the determining factor. The most defining experiences of people's lives often have little to do with their social or economic conditions. A child who loses both parents in a car crash at the age of eight faces a kind of tragedy that cannot be translated into money terms. Even if there is no worsening of her economic circumstances, that child's life is likely to be more disturbed, less secure, less happy than it would otherwise have been. A woman who is raped may live the rest of her life in fear of strangers and distrust of sexual relationships. In either case, we might talk of the 'unfairness' of life, but we would not normally use the language of equality or inequality. Nor would we normally employ such language in describing some of the happier events in our lives: the good fortune through which we stumble into a job that suits us; the great good fortune through which we meet the partner we love. In comparisons between one life and another, the biggest differences often have little to do with social status or income or wealth. Some people just turn out luckier than others, and while we can compensate in certain ways for some of life's misfortunes, there is no strictly material compensation for being born deaf, never falling in love, or losing one's parents in a car crash.

We cannot legislate against all accidents of birth or all occasions of good and bad luck, and to this extent are stuck with some inevitable level of inequality. It may seem unfair, to follow a line of argument much loved by Robert Nozick,[39] that an individual born with a Grecian profile should have a better sex life than an individual born with a snub nose. But if the only way to deal with this is to allocate sexual partners at random, we would hardly be happy with the solution. It may also seem unfair that those with a gift for communication should be better placed to influence decisions than those who find it hard to articulate their opinions. But if the only way to eliminate this is to end all political discussion, we would regard the remedy as worse than the disease. What, then, makes economic injustice so special? If people must learn to live with certain kinds of inequality, why get so agitated about those that happen to be economic in form?

Since we cannot legislate against all accidents of birth or all occasions of good and bad luck, there is always going to be a question mark over how much importance to attach to economic equality, and this will apply even setting aside pragmatic arguments about what is needed to keep a market society going and growing. Reason may suggest to us that something is absurd, illogical, indefensible. Reason should certainly alert us to the gross inconsistency in founding a social order on principles of merit and then rewarding people for qualities that come to them through no merit of their own. There is no logic in a system of rewards that talks of incentives but attaches most pay to the most enjoyable jobs; or talks of meritocracy but pays out more to people who happen to be born with a particular genetic configuration. But there is no logic in so much of human existence, no justification for the way some people are destroyed by tragedy while others live long, fulfilled lives. The power of the argument lies in the moment when it resonates with other convictions – and it is the convictions about political equality that turn out crucial here. People have learnt to live with many inequalities, have come to regard some of them as unavoidable, others as bearable, and generally tried to free themselves from the disabling resentment that comes with endlessly comparing one person's condition to another's. Nobody wants to live out a life in a permanent state of grievance. (This is why the sufficiency argument, which I find so cavalier in its attitude to unjust inequalities, none the less has such strong appeal.) The key question, for most people, is not just what is wrong (this is usually a very large category) but which wrongs most cry out for remedy; and it is entirely possible to regard the current distribution of economic resources as arbitrary or unfair without considering it a priority for change. It is when those economic inequalities contradict cherished political equalities that the sense of wrong will become more urgent.

I began this chapter with Thomas Nagel's comment that there

might still be something wrong with large economic inequalities even if they did not threaten political, legal or social equality. This is an important observation. If we do not allow for economic equality to matter in itself, we treat it as something that has no independent justification but can only be smuggled in through the back door as a means to some other end. This makes too little of economic inequalities, which can do terrible harm to people even when they have no appreciable effect on the exercise of political rights. And yet in isolating economic from political equality, I seem to do what most of this book is warning against: to compartmentalize economic from political equality and consider each as an issue apart. This generates an argument but not yet a reason for acting, for it is always possible to shrug one's shoulders at yet another of life's many unfairnesses. When people make an exception for economic inequality, it is first, because they have come to think it more amenable to change than some of life's other misfortunes; and secondly, because the gross inequalities in economic circumstances clash too harshly with the supposed equalities of their political life. These are the connections to which I now turn. The commitment to political equality sets limits to economic inequality; it also makes us less willing to put up with otherwise bearable inequalities. Though they may have been temporarily forgotten, these connections are reasonably well rehearsed in respect of class. Do they get weaker or stronger in the move from class or occupational inequalities to differences by gender, ethnicity or race?

4
From Access to Recognition

Economic equality matters for political equality in two ways: one to do with access, the other with recognition. The first reminds us that many people have restricted access to political channels: that the daily struggle with poverty leaves them no time for political activity; or that the unequal distribution of political resources (money, education, contacts, time) leaves them little hope of influencing political decisions. There is self-evident inequality when it comes to the chances of being elected to representative assemblies, and one only has to look at the social composition of legislative chambers for confirmation of this. But quite apart from its impact on elite formation, economic inequality can also prevent citizens from making equal use of their right to participate in politics. Availability of disposable time is one key element here, and in societies that allocate to women the primary responsibility for children (that is, all societies), there is a predictable gender gap in levels of political participation coinciding with the peak period of child-bearing and child-rearing. Access to politicians is another important element, for even if citizens devoted identical amounts of time to political activity, those who enjoy close contacts with the political elite (perhaps through shared trajectories of education and employment) will get a greater pay-off from their activity. More insidious than either of these is the profound difference in people's sense of political competence arising from their position in the social division of labour. One of the standard themes in the literature on participatory democracy is that those working in routinized manual employment have reduced opportunities for making decisions or exercising choice, and that this can translate into a lower sense of political efficacy.[1] Citizens in professional or managerial positions then have a built-in advantage when it comes to influencing political decisions.

All this is pretty obvious, and the commonsense perception is confirmed by studies in political participation that show levels of activism and influence to be shaped by economic resources. 'More education tends to mean more participation',[2] and while wealth has a less marked effect than educational qualifications, the wealthy turn out to be particularly forward when it comes to contacting representatives and officials and pressing their own point of view.[3] The hope of pluralist democracy was that this empowerment of the already powerful would meet some counter-force in the collective organization of the less privileged, and when trade union membership was more extensive, there was a certain balancing out of the influence, at least for men in unionized jobs. But there has never been equality in political participation. There has never been anything approaching equality in political representation. And even if we could imagine a scenario in which economic inequalities no longer affected an individual's chances of acting effectively in politics, there would still be those bastions of economic power that exert disproportionate influence on the formation of public policy.

The empirical evidence is overwhelming, and with the partial exception of voting (though this too is often skewed in favour of the wealthy), no one seriously pretends that citizens enjoy equality of political influence. Many none the less choose to ignore the discrepancy, and there are two standard justifications they draw on in their defence of the status quo. The first is that the measures required to remedy it would be too intrusive: that states would have to intervene against the freedoms of the market, and that the greater equality in participation would then be purchased only at the price of more coercion. This argument dogmatically asserts the priority of property rights over political ones, and is only persuasive if one takes this priority for granted. The other common justification is that inequalities in political influence arise out of a multiplicity of causes, and that tackling those rooted in economic conditions would still leave significant inequalities. Some people like argument, others prefer consensus;

some find their greatest fulfilment through their work life or family, others only feel themselves alive when they are engaged on a public stage. Even among those who share what Hannah Arendt called a taste for public freedom, there are qualities that will affect the contribution to political life: the capacity to make an inspiring speech, chair a meeting, remember all the details, distinguish details from the underlying point. The distribution of these qualities will be influenced by inequalities in education and the different skills we learn through our working lives, but even if we were to eliminate that class bias, there would still be differences of personality or ability that make some individuals more persuasive than others. Wherever there is politics, there is going to be inequality of political influence. Wherever there is discussion, some people are going to have a greater effect.

The only way to guarantee a strict equality of influence is to end political discussion. Those who loathe politics might find this an attractive prospect, but it is clearly incoherent to make political equality depend on eliminating politics *per se*. This is a fair enough point. But the idea that one does nothing because one cannot do everything has never struck me as persuasive, and the fact that some differences will persist is not an argument against tackling those within our control. There is no genetic reason why the taste or capacity for politics should be less developed in the poor than the rich, in one sex rather than another, or more prominent in members of whichever ethnic group happens to make up the numerical majority. If it none the less emerges that certain groups are statistically less likely to affect public decisions, it has to be because of the social factors at play: discrimination, of course, but more commonly and insidiously, the allocation of certain groups of people to roles and occupations that make it harder for them to assert their political skills or political authority.

That discrimination should be eliminated goes almost without saying. Any society claiming the title of democracy should ensure that people are not denied positions of political influence because of associations attached to their sex, class or race. This is still a pretty limited project, however, aimed at overt exclusions that have been (and still are) practised against the 'wrong kind' of people. These initiatives matter, but they do not do much to tackle those more general inequalities that reflect what have become 'real' social differences. Everyone ought to be able to contribute to the deliberations of a jury, but it is not just discrimination that stops those with fewer educational qualifications or a limited political experience outside the household from swaying the political meeting or being selected as candidates for political office. Nor is it just discrimination that makes some people less active than others. Very often, it is the lesser confidence that people have in themselves (or in the political system) because of their social position.

Such arguments recall an older socialist charge about democracy being incompatible with capitalism, and given current expectations about some form of capitalism being with us for any foreseeable future, might suggest that political equality is just a utopian dream. More usefully (and more in tune with current pronouncements by centre-left parties), such arguments ought to suggest the importance of substantive social mobility: breaking the harsh logic that requires women but not men to spend a major part of their adult lives in unpaid employment in the household; allocates people with black skins to unemployment or routinized manual labour; or condemns children from working-class families to occupations that reduce their chances of exerting political power. We cannot hope to eliminate all differences in economic circumstances. We can, more plausibly, hope to abolish those *permanent* hierarchies that put people for life into one kind of group. Philip Green (who is unusual in addressing hierarchies in reproduction as well as those in production) regards the division between mental and manual labour as the villain of this piece, for it is this that makes it impossible for certain kinds of workers to exercise their political capabilities and turns their political participation into an episodic or non-existent affair.[4] (This analysis is less convincing in societies that have a strong tradition of trade union organization or political party mobilization, where political involvement will not be limited to those in professional or white-collar jobs.) It may be that hierarchy of some sort is inevitable, and that some occupations will always be more favourable than others in promoting people's political confidence or political weight. It should still be possible to make social – and thereby political – mobility more real.

A lifetime's access to education and training figures large in Green's vision; shared parenting, combined with better social

support for those caring for young children, is the crucial addition that would get women included as well. It is clearly not
enough to give people a chance through their school years, for
the opportunity to move from one class location to another
should not be restricted to the first twenty years of life. Many
years ago, it was decided to abolish the eleven-plus examination
that sorted British children out at the age of eleven into those
who would succeed and those who would fail. (This sorting
process has now crept back in.) It is somewhat less punitive to
leave the division till the age of eighteen or twenty, but even this
is pretty destructive of development in later life. This is a point
frequently made in discussions of equal opportunity, where it is
widely argued that the chance to move between one occupation
and another should be treated not as a one-off but as a lifetime
affair. We can reach this conclusion from considerations of economic justice alone, but the argument is powerfully reinforced
when we add the political implications as well. People are still
sorted out at an early age into building workers and secretaries
and barristers, and are typically left in these categories for most
of the remainder of their lives. This is not just something that
affects future incomes and conditions of work. It also has direct
consequences for the exercise of political equality.

A society that lays claims to principles of political equality is
obliged to take social mobility very seriously, for occupation
spells political as well as market access, and the jobs people do
affect their political weight. Note, however that this is less a
matter of the distribution of income than one of the distribution
of occupation, for when equalizing political participation and
access is at issue, the key questions seem to revolve around the
kind of work people do rather than the income they derive from
it.[5] It is the argument from recognition rather than access that
has the more direct implication for income distribution. The
other point to note about access arguments is that they threaten
to become rather patronizing, for they present political activism
as dictated by economic circumstances and suggest that people
never break out of their class or occupational mould. When economic equality is presented as a condition for political equality,
this produces a neat case for more economic equality: you told us
we could be politically equal, but if that's your objective, you'd
better give us economic equality as well. Taken to its logical con-

clusion, however, the argument implies that the economically disadvantaged cannot be politically effectual and must await some saviour from on high (Rousseau's law-giver, Rawls's constitutional convention) to establish the necessary conditions. Arguments about access make an important link between political and economic equality, but do not yet get to the heart of questions about equal human worth.

Equal human worth

Political equality presumes that all individuals are, in some important respect, of equal worth. Without this presumption, it is no more than the concession previous elites made to the democratic aspirations of the masses, a bowing to the inevitable without any real conviction that those masses had right on their side. As a description of the way universal suffrage was won, 'bowing to the inevitable' is close enough to the truth, for political rights were never conceded without a struggle, and in the moment of enfranchisement, the newly admitted members of the political community were still widely regarded as trespassers on some other group's domain. The political culture of liberal democracies requires lip-service to notions of equal worth, and certainly makes it difficult for groups to mobilize under a banner of disenfranchising those deemed too lowly to justify their 'right' to a vote. (Charles Taylor notes that 'even the adversaries of extending voting rights to blacks in the Southern states found some pretext consistent with universalism, such as "tests" to be administered to would-be voters at the time of registration.')[6] But a gentle scratching of the surface often reveals deeply rooted assumptions about some people counting more than others: a disdain for the poor as activated by an unthinking politics of envy, or exaggerated respect for the rich and successful, whose achievements in the sphere of money-making are somehow thought to give them a superior understanding of public affairs.

At this point we can link political equality more directly to an equalization of incomes, addressing the economic conditions that undermine or sustain equality of respect. In the standard contrast between 'formal' and 'real' equality, the key issue is whether removing official barriers to entry really does give citizens equal access to political channels, or whether the lack of political resources still makes it impossible for people to make equal use of their supposedly equal rights. In the further emphasis on what is necessary to sustain notions of equal worth, access is complemented by recognition. It is not just that the routinized nature of so many people's working lives deprives them of the opportunity to exercise their decision-making capabilities, or that the daily confrontations with poverty leave them no time for political life. The deeper problem is that the disparity between rich and poor blocks the recognition of equal worth. Whether each has equal access to political influence – an equal chance of exerting political weight – then appears as just the tip of the iceberg. What really threatens the *Titanic* of liberal democracy is the profound lack of social recognition.

The first part of this relates to the way a society meets people's basic welfare needs, and the political difference between safety nets and universal entitlement. Any humane society would seek to ensure that nobody starved to death, but it might choose to do this under a rubric of charity; it might even promote the idea that the poor have been sent by heaven to test out the compassion and humanity of the rich. In the development of a democratic political culture, notions of charity and compassion should give way to a more egalitarian insistence on rights. It should not be a matter of the compassionate rich being incapable of living with the suffering of others, but of these others sharing with their fellow citizens the same set of entitlements and rights. In a recent recuperation of Marshall's analysis of the connection between civil, political and social rights, Desmond King and Jeremy Waldron stress that the 'concept of a citizen is that of a person who can hold her or his head high and participate fully and with dignity in the life of her or his society'.[7] This implies a linkage between citizenship and welfare rights; in their view, it also suggests that welfare should be regarded as a universal entitlement rather than a safety net to relieve the worst of the poverty. Humanity alone requires a society to provide its members with a sufficiency of resources. Democracy suggests something more. A society premised on citizen equality is poorly served by welfare policies that target the poor as objects of compassion and treat them as a category apart, and this generates a specifically political case for universal entitlement and provision.

The second element relates to the overall distribution of income, and the incompatibility of status equality with extremes of poverty and wealth. David Miller argues that social equality is more important to people than economic equality: what riles people most about inequalities in income distribution is not that the rich have finer cars or more wonderful holidays, but that the inequalities can 'crystallize into judgements of overall personal worth'.[8] He sees segregation as the real problem in this: the way that large income differentials can enable people to live such different styles of life and associate socially only with people like themselves. What possible community can the rich feel with the poorer members of their society when their wealth enables them to live in near total isolation, when the streets they live on are untainted by public housing, when their children are educated in separate schools, and when they never experience the proximity of fellow citizens in public hospitals, parks, travelling on public transport? Differences in income and life-style may not make it impossible to regard others as equals, but the capacity to view them in this way is seriously compromised by lack of contact. If this lack of contact turns out to be one of the consequences of extreme income differentials, there is a strong political case for reducing inequalities of income and wealth. Miller proposes a maximum differential of eight to one between top and bottom incomes.

The substantive thesis in this is that segregation discourages the capacity to view others as equals. It might be objected that it is proximity to those different from ourselves that resurrects long-buried ideas about social superiority and social inferiority, and that it is easier to conceive of others as your equals when you are not exposed to the details of their lives. But what this reveals, if anything, is the limited purchase of abstract ideas of human equality, for if these can so easily dissolve in the face of recalcitrant experience, they are not such a great protection. Richard Rorty has argued that literature is more powerful than philosophy in promoting a sense of common humanity, and that the skills it develops of imaginative identification do far more to 'extend our sense of "we" to people we have previously thought of as "they" '.[9] David Miller's point about what gets lost when people no longer rub shoulders with one another in schools or hospitals or shopping precincts provides a material counterpart to this, and better expresses the processes through which we come to recognize one another's humanity than any abstract assertion about the essential equality of all human beings. Claiming that we are all equal in the sight of God, or that we all share in a universal human nature, have been powerful weapons in the struggle to establish a more egalitarian society, but it is only when these ideas have entered more deeply into the way we view one another that they have had their full effect. Increased contact with others remains one of the main solvents of stereotypical misrepresentations. Failing that contact, our ideas of basic human equality can wear dangerously thin.

As a system for organizing elections and governments, democracy seems able to survive almost any gap in income and wealth, but as a deeper claim about equal human worth, it is contradicted by large economic inequalities. Because it rests on and reinforces deep notions of human equality, democracy also brings the injustices of the economic system into sharper relief, shifting these from the category of irritants that can still be tolerated to an affront on human dignity and worth. (I depart here from David Miller, who gives more credence than I do to arguments from merit and therefore has a smaller category of unjustified economic inequalities.) Democracy only makes sense if people are, in some significant sense, equals; the experience of living in even the 'thinnest' of democracies encourages people to regard that equality as a more substantive affair. In this sense, conservative fears about the democratic way of life are entirely justified: democracies do subvert the hierarchical family, undermine the 'natural' authority of religious leaders, politicians and teachers, and make it hard for anyone to exact unquestioning obedience or submission. Democracies also make people less willing to accept the privileges of birth and inheritance and more sensitive to unfairness in the economic sphere. I have suggested that one could generate an impeccable argument about the unfairness of a particular distribution of economic rewards but still have trouble making it stick: that it might be possible, for example, to establish that it is unfair for some to have more than others just because of their luck in the natural lottery, and yet because some people *are* luckier than others in all kinds of unanticipated ways, still leave a question mark over how much this unfairness matters. Linked to the promise of democracy, those arguments about economic justice become more compelling. If a society has committed itself to the principle of equal intrinsic worth, and this principle is undercut by a certain distribution of economic rewards, something has to give. Political equality then becomes a reason for economic equalization, rather than a separate concern.

All three points – that political equality implies universal welfare entitlements rather than means-tested targeting of the poor; that it is incompatible with gross discrepancies of income and wealth; and that it brings the injustices of the economic system into sharper relief – depend on questions of recognition. These arguments are, in my view, even more powerful than those that rely on access, for while differences in occupation, education or income clearly affect access to politics, the really strong case for redistribution depends on what it means to recognize others as equals. The problem for democracy is not just how to equalize people's political resources but how to establish their equal human worth; the problem with economic inequality is not just that it constrains the exercise of political rights but that it shapes (and damages) perceptions of fellow citizens.

This argument fits within a general movement from access to recognition that has been characteristic of much recent political thought, but it does so in a way that reinforces rather than weakens connections between political and economic equality. So far, however, I have looked only at the relationship between income and social status, and considered the lack of respect that can arise between groups defined by economic location. What happens to the argument when we turn to claims for recognition that are less self-evidently rooted in economic conditions – claims for equality of respect, for example, between groups defined by their ethnicity, religion or language? At this point, the movement from access to recognition suggests a more decisive break with economic concerns. As the emphasis shifts to the dangers of one-sided assimilation and the problems of misrecognition, links between the political and the economic can become particularly tenuous.

Misrecognition and cultural domination

One example that often surfaces in discussions of this is Islam. Many countries in the Western world now contain significant Muslim minorities, but even where these enjoy full rights of citizenship, there is considerable disquiet about whether the citizenship is as equal as it pretends. Not, in most of the literature, because Muslim minorities may suffer from economic disadvantages that render their political equality an empty phrase. The worry, rather, is that the liberal settlement is proving less even-handed than it imagined itself to be. Thus, countries that have adopted a strong principle of secularism may regard this as an egalitarian solution to the differences between religious groups: the state will not favour one religion over another, and will demonstrate this by establishing a strong separation between church and state. But as interpreted in the French tradition of secularism, this turned out to mean that Muslim schoolgirls were to be prohibited from wearing headscarves to school. This prohibition generated intense discussion about whether secularism was as even-handed as it claimed to be. At the simplest level, why should Christian schoolgirls be allowed to wear a symbol of their religion (crucifixes around their necks) and a similar dispensation be denied to Muslim schoolgirls? At a deeper level, why should anyone be required to suspend her religious identity in order to function as an equal citizen? Why should equality be premised on assimilation, or require people to relegate their religion to a private sphere?

French citizens of Algerian origin experience the usual disadvantages in employment and housing visited on migrants from poorer countries, but the questions raised have related to their status as citizens rather than their economic conditions. In the case of the Québécois (another widely discussed example), the link with economics is considerably more tenuous. When Charles Taylor writes of the harm done to the French-speaking Québécois by the failure to respect or recognize their collective concerns, he focuses on the threat posed to their cultural and linguistic identity by an encroaching pan-Canadian norm. The harm can be linked historically to patterns of economic disadvantage that kept the province of Quebec a rural backwater within a rapidly industrializing Canada, and enabled English-speaking

Canadians to establish a temporary hegemony over industrial and commercial life. But those economic inequalities have long been erased, and the strong assertion of a distinctively Québécois identity occurred just at the moment of economic convergence. If it is none the less plausible to talk of a lack of respect or failure of recognition – a failure, that is, in the deeper meaning of political equality – these no longer correlate in any obvious way with inequalities in economic conditions.

Recent results from a survey of ethnic minorities in Britain suggest a similar decoupling of material disadvantage from cultural (in this case, racial) inequality for at least some minority groups.[10] On a range of economic indicators relating to income, qualifications, housing, and employment, it no longer makes much sense to describe African Asians (those whose families were expelled from Kenya and Uganda in the late 1960s or early 1970s) or the Chinese as economically disadvantaged groups; and while Pakistanis and Bangladeshis are still seriously and consistently disadvantaged, those of Caribbean and Indian origin are edging closer towards parity with the white population. None of these groups, however, comes close to equity with the white majority in terms of political influence or political representation, and all continue to be exposed to racial abuse and attacks. In their reflections on this, many members of minority groups have come to regard economic disadvantage as only one part of the picture; equally oppressive is the arrogant assimilationism that welcomes strangers into the fold only when they abandon their markers of difference. Hence the importance now attached to securing political representation for members of minority groups. Hence, also, the importance of securing equal respect and recognition for minority cultural practices, and the theorization of a multicultural citizenship that accommodates differences between citizens rather than expecting minorities to abandon their own practices and norms.

Racism undoubtedly feeds on economic inequality, as when those forced to live in over-crowded and poorly maintained slums are said to have lower standards of personal hygiene, or when those exposed to higher rates of unemployment are said to be more irresponsible than the rest. A stark difference in material conditions engenders disrespect (these people are not really like us) and fear (I do not understand these people, I cannot predict what they are likely to do). But neither the disrespect nor the fear will necessarily dissolve when there is greater convergence in economic conditions. They may, more probably, dissolve if there is a convergence in culture as well as in income, but in such cases the equality of respect is being gained at the price of difference: I no longer despise you because you have become like me in every conceivable way. It is hard to sustain any sense of superiority over people who have had the same education, talk the same language, enjoy the same music, bring up their children in exactly the same way. When the only remaining difference is in the colour of our skin, there is no reference point for racial claims. But the recognition that is achieved through convergence falls a long way short of what is implied in equal respect, and this is particularly so when the convergence is only one-way. If I can respect only those who are like me, the only person I respect is myself.

The first point suggested by these examples is that there are patterns of domination, denial, or exclusion that are independent of economic disadvantage: forms of oppression that significantly undermine the promise of political equality but have little or nothing to do with economic conditions. For those reared in a more materialist framework, the first hurdle to overcome is acknowledging that there are harms we do to one another that are independent in this way: nastinesses that have no economic rationality; hatreds that have no reference point in material conflicts of interest; dislikes that arise out of thin air. In a world teeming with ethnic and religious conflict, it might seem odd that anyone would find this difficult. But the world is also created out of countless interconnections, and it can be hard to isolate any one element from the others. I would hazard a guess that any group that becomes a focus of resentment or object of disparagement will turn out to differ on some scale of economic comparison: to be more heavily concentrated, perhaps, in certain occupations than others, or more likely to live in a particular part of town. The differences may have receded into history, but even in cases where one can talk of a decoupling of material from cultural disadvantage, there will still be a history of economic difference. Or the differences may have been forced on people by a discrimination that closed down alternatives, as when ethnic minority groups have higher than average home ownership (after their humiliating experiences in trying to find properties to rent), or higher than average levels of self-employment (after being refused access to the normal range of jobs). In these cases, one might want to argue that the economic differences are not so much cause as effect. They are still there as part of what generates a sense of group difference, and can still be a crucial element in destroying relationships of equal respect.

In her analysis of the dynamic between struggles for redistribution and struggles for recognition, Nancy Fraser agrees that it is virtually impossible to separate out pure instances of economic domination from pure instances of cultural domination, for in practice these are always closely enmeshed. She none the less insists on an analytical distinction. There are some injustices that are rooted in the political-economic structure of society: exploitation, economic marginalization, and the starker deprivation that deprives people of an adequate standard of living. The remedy for these lies in what Fraser terms redistribution – a redistribution of income, reorganization of the division of labour, democratization of investment decisions, and transformation of basic economic structures. Cultural injustices, by contrast, are rooted in the cultural or symbolic order: the domination that subjects members of one cultural group to patterns of interpretation and communication that are associated with an alien and/or hostile culture; the misrecognition of one's own cultural understandings so often associated with this; the routine malignment, disparagement, disrespect that is dealt out to people because of their sexuality, gender or race. Though the latter injustices very often coexist with the former (most notably, in the case of women and racial minorities), she argues that they have to be recognized as having a distinct dynamic of their own. Most importantly, they have to be seen as demanding different remedies: not just the redistribution that tackles the specifically economic injustices but the recognition that accords people an equality of respect.

The illustrations Fraser provides suggest a continuum that runs from those groups who experience primarily cultural domination to those who experience primarily economic domination, and includes a number of groups characterized by a combination of these two: lesbians and gay men at one extreme, women and blacks in the middle, the working class and poor at the other extreme. This categorization lays Fraser open to criticism for failing to acknowledge the economic disadvantages associated with homosexuality (discrimination in taxation, for example, or pension rights)[11] as well as the cultural domination associated with class (the disparagement of working-class life-styles, or the relationship between status and accent). But these can be seen as minor qualifications, for her key point is that it does not help to see everything as interconnected, or use this to absolve one from determining what is more 'cultural' from what is more 'economic'.

There is a powerful strand in contemporary theory that refuses to make these distinctions, that prefers to define political economy as cultural, culture as economic, or employs a quasi-Marxist analysis of the mode of production to establish that gender and sexuality are crucial to the production and reproduction of material life.[12] The first falls into what Fraser describes as an argument by definition, while the second is overtly functionalist,[13] and neither makes it easy to address patterns of cultural domination that might be in tension with or autonomous of the structures of economic life. Fraser is not proposing a total separation: she talks of 'even the most material economic institutions' as having 'a constitutive, irreducible cultural dimension', and 'even the most discursive cultural practices' as having 'a constitutive, irreducible political-economic dimension'.[14] But if we do not allow for at least some analytic distinction, we fail to grasp the conflicts, tensions and dilemmas that can arise between the two. If we treat them as part of a monolithic system (or even worse, describe the one as causing the other), we may also fail to recognize that each has an equal claim.

On this reading of the relationship between the cultural and the economic, the fact that patterns of cultural domination may have come into existence in association with patterns of economic domination is not decisive. There may or may not have been a historical connection, but even if there were, we cannot assume that the one is subsumed in the other. Fraser's analysis derives from what she describes as 'a quasi-Weberian dualism of status and class',[15] and an insistence on the distinctively status injuries that arise out of being denied the status of full partner in social interaction or being prevented from participating as a full equal in social life. If I understand her argument correctly, the status injuries associated with heterosexism, racism or sexism may well have emerged in association with particular patterns of economic domination. There is still an injury here that is distinct from the economic injury and is open to remedy outside the economic sphere. This makes things simultaneously more open and closed: 'The good news is that we do not need to overthrow capitalism in order to remedy these disabilities . . . the bad news is that we need to transform the existing status order and restructure the relations of recognition.'[16]

Transforming a status order is clearly a different kind of task from transforming an economic hierarchy, and one can think of a number of initiatives that might fall into this category. Rewriting the curriculum pursued in schools or universities has been seen as one important focus, for while rewriting history texts to highlight the role of women or the contribution of migrant communities or the treatment of indigenous peoples does little to change their respective economic conditions, it can challenge previous misrepresentations and significantly enhance the capacity to view others as equals. The official redefinition of a country as multi-ethnic and multicultural does not guarantee economic equality between ethnic groups, but it begins to detach citizenship from unstated association with the dominant ethnic group, opening up space for the recognition of others. Changing the way key events in a nation's history are celebrated (Columbus's arrival in America, for example) modifies, in however small a way, the existing status order. Extending to lesbian or gay couples some of the rights enjoyed by heterosexual couples not only challenges an inequitable distribution of privileges but accords new public recognition to homosexuals.

I have already discussed some of the objections raised against claims to group recognition: that they may privilege one group over another, or privilege group concerns over individual rights. The question I address now is whether initiatives associated with recognition claims exaggerate the role of the political or cultural, thereby contributing to a lack of concern with inequalities in economic life. The marked shift from a discourse of racism to one of multiculturalism, for example, can be regarded as a belated acknowledgment that racism has as much to do with the failure to recognize the legitimacy of difference as with starker statistics about employment or housing or poverty. But the turn towards questions of recognition can also look like displacement. It may encourage us to think that contestations about the content of the educational curriculum substitute for campaigns to equalize access to decent schools. It has certainly encouraged political theorists to focus on groups who experience cultural (rather than economic) injury as the paradigmatic examples of oppression and inequality: to focus on ethnicity rather than race, and within the definition of an ethnic group, to focus on culture and religion rather than location in power relations.

The shift towards questions of recognition may then move the conditions for democratic equality out of the economic and into an exclusively political or cultural sphere. The earlier focus on class divisions directed attention to the distribution of incomes and occupations and the way structural inequalities in power thwart the promise of political equality. The subsequent focus on inequalities associated with gender, ethnicity, religion, language or race has generated strategies more specifically directed at political or legal arrangements, and this can give the impression that equality of citizenship is to be achieved exclusively through changes in these. I have argued that we should indeed dispense with a cruder 'base–superstructure' metaphor that treats the political as a mere reflection of the economic, and have welcomed the turn towards politics as opening up questions closed down in earlier debates. I none the less believe that many of the questions relating to recognition can be fully addressed only in association with changes in economic relations: that they arise most forcibly where groups have experienced structural inequalities in economic conditions; and that they cannot be finally resolved outside changes in these conditions. On this point, I differ from those who treat recognition struggles as logically distinct.

Assimilation and convergence

One way of approaching this is to ask whether inequalities can be remedied through convergence, and if so, whether that includes convergence in economic conditions. Economic inequality is almost by definition dealt with in this way, for if the problem lies in the exaggerated discrepancy between rich and poor, the answer is to reduce the range. Inequalities between cultural groups do not fit this paradigm so neatly: if the problem lies in a lack of respect for what is distinctive and different, it is hardly going to be solved by destroying all distinctions. Converting everyone to Christianity is self-evidently dishonest as a way of achieving religious equality, but there are also problems with convergence on a religious Esperanto that takes elements from each of the world's religions and welds them into some homogeneous whole. The second fantasy is more egalitarian (it could be said to be equally disrespectful to every religion), but if the equality is to be achieved only by abolishing all difference, it is an equality hardly worthy of the name.

There is, however, a difference between assimilation and convergence, and the criticisms that hold of the first do not always apply to the second. Assimilationist strategies have had a long history within feminism, where it has often been suggested that women can regain their self-respect and raise their social valuation by participation in the previously male world of work, and that they will make themselves equals by breaking into the previously 'male' spheres of education, employment and politics. The difficulty with this is that the equality then depends on eliminating what has made women different from men. Many have regarded this as an unhealthy capitulation to dominant values and norms. The counter-position (also with a long history in feminism) asks why women should be required to simulate the activities of men in order to be recognized as equals. Why is assimilation the necessary condition for equality? Why is the convergence always one-way?

The strong version of this (particularly associated with what has come to be called cultural feminism) suggests that men and women can be equal though different, that there are indeed intrinsic differences between the sexes, and that equality lies not in convergence but in a revaluation of traditionally female qualities or roles. The weaker version accepts some kind of convergence as a condition for equality, but asks why it is always women who have to emulate male qualities and never the other way round. In the medium term, at least, there may be little to distinguish these positions. Both call for a revaluation of the activities or qualities conventionally associated with women: a recognition, for example, that the work of caring for others is as vital as the production of commodities for sale, or that the supposedly inferior capacity for empathy is as crucial to human well-being as the capacity for applying impersonal rules. The weaker version believes that the revaluation will remain partial and superficial until men and women become more genuinely interchangeable in their social and parenting roles. It is weaker, not in the sense of being less demanding about the scale of the required transformation, but in accepting convergence in material conditions as a necessary grounding for equality of respect. The strong version may seem to ask less, for it anticipates continuing differences between men and women in the relationships they develop with their children or the kinds of job they typically do. It does, however, represent a more challenging critique of the convergence model. To that extent, it is closer to some of the arguments that have been developed about the recognition of cultural minorities or the respect that should be accorded to different ethnic or religious groups.

As far as sexual inequalities are concerned, what I have called the weaker version is the more persuasive. This is so for two reasons: the ambiguity that necessarily surrounds notions of 'women's culture'; and the difficulty of establishing a full equality of respect between the sexes if they continue to be markedly different in their activities and roles. The idea that women require recognition for their distinct and different culture grossly overstates the homogeneity of 'women's culture'. It also presumes that the characteristics that have come to be associated with women's way of thinking or women's way of being are ones we will want to sustain and protect, in much the same way as one might want to sustain and protect minority cultures from forced assimilation into majority values. As far as women's culture is concerned, this strikes me as a dubious presumption. I readily acknowledge that there are differences between women and men. Given the markedly different treatment of boys and girls as they grow up, not to mention the markedly different roles then allocated to them in carework, relationships and employment, it would be distinctly odd if both sexes turned out the same. For this to be the outcome, people would have to be extraordinarily immune to the social influences acting upon them: inhuman, almost, in their detachment from social conditions. But I cannot see that differences that derive from historical inequalities or relationships of power and subordination can be treated as objects of veneration, differences one would seek to sustain.

Femininity and masculinity alike are tainted by the processes that create them, and neither, in my view, is entitled to the kind of respect that might more legitimately be accorded to traditions that have developed over centuries inside aboriginal communities, or traditions that migrant groups bring with them from their countries of origin. 'Women's culture' has been formed in relations of dependency and subordination, and what is positive within it – the caring, the empathy, the capacity to puncture male pomposity and pretensions – is almost inextricably intertwined with aspects that are less attractive. (One of Simone de Beauvoir's complaints about women was that they were particularly prone to 'bad faith': living in conditions of relative powerlessness, they were always inclined to blame other people or fate for the things that went wrong in their lives.) I have enough sympathy with feminist standpoint theory to think that 'men's culture' is even more thoroughly deformed, and that the traditions of solidarity developed among women give 'women's culture' the edge in any comparative critique. But since each culture is defined in relation to the other, it is hard to envisage a successful challenge to masculinity that does not transform its feminine counterpart. Neither master nor slave generates a model culture; challenging the one inevitably involves challenging the other.

This part of my argument overlaps closely with the position developed by Nancy Fraser. Fraser argues that women will be better served by recognition strategies that are deconstructive rather than affirmative, that destabilize, that is, fixed gender identities, break down conventional distinctions between male and female, and allow for the free elaboration of many kinds of difference. This is far more promising, she suggests, than the simpler affirmation of women's distinct and valuable culture, which 'insistently calls attention to, if it does not performatively create, women's putative cultural specificity or difference'.[17] Fraser sees the affirmative strategy as particularly misguided because of the backlash it so often generates; I see it as misguided because of the exaggerated respect it accords to 'women's culture'; we agree on the general point. My second argument is more at odds with Fraser's analytic distinction between economic and cultural injustice, for I also want to say that cultural vilification cannot be remedied through cultural intervention alone.

This second point is more a matter of guesswork about the conditions that can sustain genuine equality of respect. One of the points anthropologists have established is that there is an extraordinary diversity between cultures when it comes to what is viewed as 'women's work' and what is viewed as 'men's'. The one depressing similarity is that the first is always regarded as less valuable than the second. Whatever the distinction, it becomes loaded with hierarchical assumptions: what women do is less worthy of respect than whatever it is that is done by the men. At an individual level, it is undoubtedly possible to respect those who are different: to admire qualities in others that are singularly lacking in yourself; or respect the choices others have made even when they are very different from your own. But what evidence we have suggests that more blanket distinctions between the sexes will always encourage notions of superiority and inferiority. I find it hard to believe that we can sustain equality of respect without greater convergence in our lives.

David Miller argues that it is hard to maintain the conviction of equal worth when excesses of poverty and wealth impose such great differences on people's lives. In similar vein, I would say it is hard to maintain the conviction of equal worth for both sexes when women and men are segregated into different occupations, and expected to act such different parts in their social and domestic lives. Sexual equality, in my view, does depend on convergence. It depends on men and women being equally distributed across all the activities and roles in society (including the labour and pleasure of caring for others) so that the difference of sex, as Mary Wollstonecraft once put it, is confounded, and we can differ as individuals rather than as representatives of a sex. Assimilation is certainly no answer, but that is because assimilation is by definition one-way. Convergence, understood as a transformation in the conditions of life for both women *and* men, is not objectionable.

When it comes to sexual equality, claims to recognition are inextricable from claims to equality of condition. This is not to say that every coherent initiative must revolve around the sexual division of labour, or that no distinction can be made between the political, cultural or economic. Initiatives relating to women's political representation intervene on a different terrain from those that deal with the portrayal of women in fiction, and this is different again from the treatment of rape victims in the law courts or the provision of childcare or women's access to a full range of jobs. That success in one may depend on further changes in another is no reason to hold back: I think democracies should adopt mechanisms of affirmative action to ensure parity of representation between the sexes, and have no patience with the idea that this must wait on more fundamental transformations in social and economic life. But the recognition claims pressed by women still remain securely attached to questions of economic equality, for the full equality of respect can only be guaranteed when there is convergence in economic and social conditions.

The relationship between the sexes is peculiar in one respect, for each sex is defined precisely through its relation to the other. Other groups are also defined through their relation to another, as when one group is given the jobs that another won't do, or when the characteristics ascribed to one culture turn out to be the mirror image of the characteristics ascribed to another, but there is no other example where the two groups are so exclusively intertwined. One might, at a stretch, say that 'black culture' is defined through its relation to 'white culture', but this would ignore the historical influences that come from people's countries of origin, and underplay the impact of official or informal segregation in generating independent cultural traditions. It would certainly be implausible to say that the culture of aboriginal peoples is formed only through the relationship to subsequent settlers, or Islam through its relationship to Christianity; and while national identities would lose their meaning if there were no other nationalities for comparison, there is never a single binary that defines country X through its relationship to country Y.

Racially defined differences come closest to sexually defined differences, for the categorizing of people by their physiognomy and skin colour only makes sense in relationships of domination and subordination. In what other context could 'race' have emerged as a significant way of dividing up the human species?

(This is the point signalled by contemporary writers who will only use the term inside inverted commas. They are not denying the very acute sense people have of themselves as black or white or brown, and certainly not denying the phenomenon of racism, but they refuse to give credence to the pseudo-scientific taxonomy that defines people according to something called their 'race'.) We might conclude that racial identities are as tainted by the processes that created them as are femininity and masculinity, and equally good candidates for deconstruction. The difficulty with this is that racial identities are not exclusively formed by the relationship to a superior or inferior 'racial' group; they can also be ethnic identities, formed around cultural or linguistic traditions that have developed in relative autonomy from the dominant group. A group that has been historically subordinate may also have generated traditions of resistance (including a strong sense of mutual assistance, or a greater reliance on the extended family) that it is determined to sustain. In these circumstances, the homogeneity implied by convergence looks neither necessary nor desirable. Why should respect be conditional on identity? Why cannot we value and respect our differences, rather than dissolving them into a mish-mash of the same?

Different kinds of difference

Assimilationism is profoundly inegalitarian, and has sometimes been practised with extraordinary cruelty. The forcible removal of up to one-third of aboriginal children in Australia between 1910 and 1970, to be fostered by white families or brought up in white missions and orphanages, is one terrible example of this. The dissolution of all cultural, religious and linguistic differences into a cosmopolitan Esperanto is less overtly inegalitarian, but also makes false claims about convergence as the condition for equality. There are different kinds of difference, and convergence is only appropriate to some of these. It would be silly to suggest that divergent belief-systems should be brought together by halving the difference, or to present religious convergence as the condition for religious equality. Uncovering the commonality between the world's major religions remains one powerful way of promoting the sense of equal worth, but there is no reason why each should dissolve into the other in order to secure equality of respect. Cultural differences are more complicated, for some of what differentiates one culture from another is the practices each pursues in relationships between men and women or parents and children. Egalitarians will (rightly) refuse to regard all cultures as equally worthy when some are less just than others in their treatment of women or girls, and in such cases egalitarians' willingness to respect another culture could be said to depend on it becoming less different from their own. However, the willingness to accord equal respect to the members of another cultural group (the members, rather than the culture) is another matter. Here, one relies on the recognition that all of us are formed by the traditions and practices of our group, and none of us has a monopoly on the truth. Since most people also value diversity (apart from a brief moment in adolescence, we like to think of ourselves as different and do not want to dissolve into a homogeneous whole), we cannot regard convergence as the only route to citizen equality.

The critique of equality as sameness does not, however, imply that *any* difference is compatible with equality. The prospects for sexual equality depend, in my view, on a substantial process of convergence between the life experiences of women and men, and as far as the economic conditions for equality of respect are concerned, there are close parallels with racial equality. In both cases, difference has been strongly overlaid with hierarchy, and it is hard to feel confident about a scenario that continues to segregate one group from the other but proclaims their essential equality. A society in which women dominate the caring professions while men run the economy is unlikely to generate the more profound sense of equal worth that underpins the principle of political equality. In similar vein, a society in which black people excel in athletics and white people in managing the banks is unlikely to do the trick. I may be overly pessimistic in my reading of the human psyche, but in cases where there has been a strong historical association between difference and inferiority, the persistent segregation in occupations and roles makes it hard to sustain strong convictions of equal worth, and the differences become incompatible with equality. We come back, in other words, to the corrosive effects of segregation when this segregation reflects differences in power, and the way that certain differences in economic condition can crystallize into judgements of inferior worth.

As far as class inequalities are concerned, there is a well-established relationship between economic and political inequality, and good reasons (arising from considerations of access and recognition alike) for regarding an equalization in economic conditions as part of the project of democratic equality. The insight from recent literature on citizenship is that there are other failures of recognition that are less intrinsically connected to economic inequality. In such cases, achieving equality of status depends on securing respect for multiple differences rather than wishing those differences away. The point I have stressed is that even beyond the directly class inequalities, there are still strong links between economic circumstances and political equality. The association of certain categories of people with certain categories of work has particularly profound effects on a society's status order, and even the most rigorous campaign of cultural revaluation is unlikely to make enough difference to this. Some of the current inequalities between citizens do lend themselves to treatment via the cultural or symbolic order. All too many of them remain attached to economic location.

Economic equality matters, and its absence has serious political effects. That said, if we make it all that matters, we can end up with a depoliticized determinism that denies any independent role to political action or political judgements. 'Given the structural tendencies towards inequalities, political action on the part of the socially and economically disadvantaged becomes the crucial means of saving themselves.'[18] This refers back to some of the earlier arguments about the importance of politics. It also refers forward to a dissatisfaction with recent literature on deliberative democracy, where 'acting to save oneself' has come to be regarded as a dubiously self-interested affair.

5
Deliberation and the Republic

I have focused so far on ways in which politics has become more prominent, and the worry this provokes about casting issues of economic equality into the shade. Some will view this as a peculiar misreading of contemporary dilemmas, and there are a number of other complaints that come in from an almost diametrically opposed direction. Politics may be all around us, but in its stronger sense of public action and civic responsibility, 'the political' can also be said to be in deep decline. In a particularly marked contrast to my argument so far, those who make this point sometimes go on to suggest that it is the very subservience to economics that is the problem. Liberal democracy has been criticized for severing political from economic equality. But liberal democracy is also criticized for turning politics into the handmaiden of the economic, reducing the activities of citizenship to the protection of individual or group self-interest, and destroying what ought to be the distinctive qualities attached to the public sphere.

The first part of this complaint is that there has been a creeping (perhaps a galloping) politicization that empties political action of its real meaning: everything has become political, with the unfortunate consequence that we lose our sense of what makes politics unique. There are various reasons why this might have happened, but some of it stems from a radicalism that has extended the meaning of politics in order to extend the range of human affairs. Definitions of politics are notoriously varied and imprecise, ranging from 'the art of compromise' and

'the conciliation of interests' to 'the pursuit of common concerns'. Sometimes they fall back on the circularity that equates
politics with what political activists and politicians do. One point
stands out clearly: that when people argue about what comes
within the scope of politics, it is because they see this as saying
something about what is amenable to human action and change.
What is political is, by implication, open to choice. Indeed, when
we describe something as presenting a political choice, the adjective is almost superfluous, the point being that the issue in question is not settled by absolute values or pre-determined by
natural laws.

The association with action and choice runs as a recurrent
thread through discussions of the nature and meaning of
politics.[1] I do not mean to suggest that people treat politics as the
realm of pure will, a sphere in which anything and everything
becomes possible. But politics has come to carry much of the
weight of what is available to human intervention, and because
of this, many of the battles over what can or cannot be altered
are fought out on the terrain of what counts as 'politics'. The
result, inevitably, has been the expansion of the category to
include more and more aspects of social life. Much of the radical
literature of this century has been devoted to exposing the lie
that certain things are outside politics: revealing the profoundly
political nature of economic forces, of the supposedly 'natural'
dichotomy between the sexes, of claims to scientific objectivity
or truth. One of the most telling ideas developed by Michel
Foucault is that the categories through which we divide up the
world operate as regimes of power, defining for us what we
can and cannot say, regulating us in the most insidious of
ways through the very discourses we employ. Some have read
this as a message of despair, for if power relations are all pervasive, it hardly seems worth replacing one set by another. But for
most of those who have pushed back the boundaries of what
counts as political, the more usual expectation is that this
enlarges the scope for human action. If there is nothing we can
designate as outside of politics, then nothing is immune to
contestation.

This radical politicization comes, however, at a price. One of
the losses we potentially sustain is the capacity to differentiate
between matters that really are political and others that are not;

the other is the disappearance of a specifically public sphere. In a provocative survey of Western political thought, Sheldon Wolin identified what he saw as 'the depreciation of the politicalness of the political order':[2] the turn from politics to a preoccupation with society, the substitution of administration for politics, and the associated decline of citizenship as a distinct sphere of activity. Classical liberalism, he argued, was not the confident rationalism that appeared in its subsequent caricatures; on the contrary, Wolin suggested, 'liberalism was a philosophy of sobriety, born in fear, nourished by disenchantment, and prone to believe that the human condition was and was likely to remain one of pain and anxiety'.[3] Attaching little confidence to what could be achieved through politics alone, liberals looked to forces generated within society and economy to sustain social cohesion. The anti-political impulse nurtured by this liberalism became all-pervasive through the nineteenth and twentieth centuries, surfacing variously in the works of the utopian socialists, Proudhon, Comte, Marx, Durkheim, the Fabians, and assorted theorists of managerialism. A distinct sphere of political – or citizen – activity was no longer considered either desirable or necessary: at best, politics only registered a more fundamental social or economic reality; at worst, it could pervert the course of human affairs. So when Lenin, for example, looked to a world in which politics would be replaced by administration, he was far more in tune with the mood of the twentieth century than his opponents have liked to believe.

Though part of his argument is that politics became subordinated to administration, Wolin also traces connections between the later politicization of everything and the disappearance of politics itself. The point he stresses is that politics dropped out just when people seemed most convinced that it was all around. It was not that people stopped talking about politics; on the contrary, they became adept at spotting political activity and phenomena everywhere, from trade unions to corporations to churches. But if everything is to be regarded as political, the adjective becomes a trivial addition, and it is rather hard to know what to do with the noun. By the middle of the twentieth century, Wolin argues, it had become virtually impossible to conceive of a distinct sphere of citizen activity in which people sought to address issues of common concern. Politics, understood as the human capacity to deal with collective concerns, had dropped from view.

Similar arguments have surfaced in recent feminist theory. When feminists claimed the personal as political, they were contesting the passivity that treated relationships between the sexes as so determined by history or biology that no one could seriously hope to fashion them in another way. In doing so, they drew attention to the power relations that shape the most intimate fabric of private life. They also developed from this a more localized understanding of politics that shifted attention from the legislative chambers or the activities of national parties to focus on the democratization of daily existence. But the questioning of distinctions between public and private has been said to lead to an over-politicization of personal and familial life, and a corresponding depoliticization of public life by woolly notions about emotion or empathy or care. On the one hand, there is an excessive policing of the choices people make about what to wear or whom to sleep with, as if each action is loaded with a world historic sense of political responsibility. On the other hand, there is a denial of what is distinctive about acting as a citizen, as if the way we relate to our loved ones can be a model for the relationship between strangers that necessarily defines political life.

When Jean Bethke Elshtain challenged what she saw as the breathtaking presumption of earlier feminist activists, she made the point that treating everything as political encourages people to believe that everything is amenable to political solution. Yet part of the struggle, she observes, 'involves reflecting on whether our current misery and unhappiness derive entirely from faulty and exploitative social forms that can, and therefore must, be changed or whether a large part of that unhappiness derives from the simple fact of being human, therefore limited, knowing that one has to die'.[4] Literal interpretations of 'the personal is political' have been widely criticized in recent years, and for many feminists, the more careful delineation of what is and isn't political has combined with a growing interest in the analysis of the public sphere.[5] One issue raised here is whether one can sensibly look to values generated within private life as the basis for a better democracy; another is whether the attention feminists have given to representing women's needs and interests undermines the capacity for developing shared concerns. Where some feminists have looked to the practices and values associated with mothering as offering a more generous model for activities in the public sphere, others have argued that the care mothers owe to their vulnerable and dependent children is crucially different from the equal engagement with others that ought to characterize public life.[6] And where some have looked to feminism to pinpoint the particular needs or interests of women, others have drawn on notions of a woman-friendly citizenship to recast the relationship between universality and difference.[7] Most feminists continue to take issue with the notion that public action is separable from private identities, or that acting as a citizen requires one to forget whether one is a woman or a man. The renewed interest in the public sphere none the less reflects widespread worries about over-politicization – and its sidekick, depoliticization – in contemporary societies.

The second part of the complaint is that liberalism reduced the role of government to the protection of private interest, thereby making politics subservient to interests in the economic sphere. As liberty came to be conceived primarily as a matter of freedom from interference, the more traditional understanding of democracy as the practice of self-government gave way to a 'protective' model of democracy as securing the rights and freedoms of individuals and groups. Politics was then downgraded into a competition between interest groups. Taking their cue from the 'hidden hand' of the market (which magically translates the autonomous actions of individual producers and consumers into a system that meets everyone's needs), people began to think of politics as the mere aggregation of preferences. I pressure the politicians to meet my interests, you pressure them to meet yours, and the politicians sensibly align themselves with whichever policies are most likely to keep them in office. No need for high-minded idealism, public acts of bravery, or conscious pursuit of a 'common good': all that is required is that each pursues his or her own interests and abides by majority rules.

This conception of politics has been contested almost from the moment of its arrival (Rousseau being one early critic), and those most irked by its shallow understanding of public action or responsibility have sometimes argued that we must get the economics out of the politics in order to restore the vitality of political life. The idea that the modern world threatens the distinctiveness of the polis has been particularly powerfully articulated by Hannah Arendt, who came to believe that public action was possible only when 'the social question' was rigorously excluded from public debate. She saw the political order as increasingly downgraded into an arena in which individuals or groups pursued narrowly economic purposes, and she saw even the more humane obsession with problems of poverty or hunger as undermining the quality of political life. When the poor 'appeared on the scene of politics, necessity appeared with them, and the result was that the power of the old regime became impotent and the new republic was stillborn; freedom had to be surrendered to necessity, to the urgency of the life process itself'.[8] Arendt was no admirer of the *ancien régime*, but she saw the very urgency attached to poverty as antithetical to politics because on poverty there was really nothing to say. The experience of poverty generates an ideal of abundance: not the freedom to engage in politics but the freedom from want and despair. As politics became devoted to what Arendt saw as the administration of economic growth, 'the individual ... got the better of the citizen'.[9] Instead of conceiving of politics as the exercise of public freedom, people came to regard political participation as a burden and government as just a necessary evil. The consequent denial of political responsibility figures prominently in Arendt's analysis of the pathology of totalitarian regimes.[10]

Contemporary versions of this are less exercised by the intrusion of Arendt's 'social question', but remain highly critical of the dominance of interest-group politics and the way this blocks deliberation on what should be matters of common concern.[11] When politics is conceived on a model of aggregation, no premium is attached to sorting things out. We do not have to bother ourselves with whether one demand is more legitimate than another, we do not have to try to understand an opponent's point of view. The fact that your preferences blatantly reflect your own group's self-interest is neither here nor there; so, after all, do mine. We add them up, we cancel one another out, we end up with a roughly majoritarian point of view. That this may tread harshly on certain minority interests is sometimes recognized as a problem; this is why countries frequently introduce qualifications to majority rule (for example, through a Bill of Rights) to prevent numerical majorities implementing legislation that discriminates against a minority. But even with such protections, this is a model of democracy that makes no high-minded claims about politics as the conscious pursuit of justice or deliberation about matters of common concern. Whoever has power wins.

The critique of this often derives from a critique of market society, and to that extent shares some of my own preoccupations about the relationship between political and economic equality. But as Arendt's work tellingly illustrates, the preferred solution is often to minimize the impact of economic issues on political decision-making and debate. If the problem is that politics has become subservient to economic interest, one obvious solution is to get those interests out of politics. Rousseau dealt with this by recommending a radical equalization in civil society: no man to be so rich that he could purchase another; none so poor that he had to sell his labour to somebody else. The more common response in the twentieth century has been to find a way of curtailing the impact of self- or group interest on public affairs: not to eliminate the clash of interests, but to make these less politically dominant. In the context of what continues to be an unequal world, this is a deeply problematic approach.

Civic republicanism

Those who regard the erosion of the specifically political as one of the more damning features of contemporary life often look to an earlier tradition of civic republicanism to counter the shallowness of liberal democracy. Born out of the democracy of the Greek city-states, revived (in rather different form) in Renaissance Italy, carried through (somewhat patchily) into the values of the American Revolution, this tradition is said to differ from the prevailing liberalism in the importance it attaches to self-government. Michael Sandel argues that in the liberal conception, 'liberty is not internally but only incidentally related to self-government'.[12] Democracy is valued only in so far as it provides the best conditions for individuals to pursue their own

interests and ends, and the best democracy is the one that does
the least. It is expected to aim at maximum neutrality between
competing moral views (no privileging of one conception of the
good over another), and it should not impose on its members too
high a burden of citizen involvement. In the republican conception, by contrast, freedom is bound up with self-government.
This not only means that republicans set a high value on public
service and political participation. It also, in Sandel's reading,
means that freedom depends on the willingness to put the
common good above private interests and concerns. The civic
virtues associated with this will stress obligations rather than
rights – what we owe to the community rather than what the
community might owe to us.

In the 'community-speak' now favoured by many policy ad-
visers and politicians, the interest in republican conceptions of
self-government is often welded on to a critique of welfare
dependency, and the inculcation of civic responsibility becomes
associated with a parallel inculcation of the responsibility to find
oneself work. (The latter is sometimes 'inculcated' in the starkest
of fashions by simply abolishing welfare payments.) Sandel indi-
cates considerable sympathy with this line of argument,[13] but he
also argues that the extremes of wealth and poverty that came to
characterize American life in the 1980s and 1990s undermine
the commonality that is necessary to self-government. Some of
the argument here recalls David Miller's critique of the segregation of rich from poor that is associated with large income differentials, the way this enables the rich to buy their way out of
public provision, and undermines perceptions of equal status.
But where I take Miller to be centrally concerned with the conditions that sustain a strong sense of each individual's equal
worth, Sandel is far more preoccupied with what promotes the
sense of a shared community. He is also less worried about the
distribution of income as such and more interested in 'class-
mixing' institutions (he lists public schools, libraries, parks,
community centres, public transportation and national service)
that help 'form the habits of citizenship'. So while he identifies
a certain political economy associated with citizenship, he
detaches this from considerations of equality and puts it onto
community instead. 'A more civic-minded liberalism would seek
communal provision less for the sake of distributive justice than

for the sake of affirming the membership and forming the civic identity of rich and poor alike.'[14]

Though this communitarian strand of civic republicanism criticizes some elements of market society, it is peculiarly ill equipped to address questions of political equality. It is less interested in what is necessary to secure equality than in what is necessary to sustain community membership. It also has little sympathy with the cultural egalitarianism that stresses the heterogeneity of contemporary societies and seeks equality of respect for a diversity of cultural groups. The one point of contact is that it too criticizes the abstentionist toleration that relegates differences to a protected private zone. But the communitarian critique is that this brackets out questions of morality, and encourages us to think that anything goes. Sandel, for example, argues that we should abandon this tolerant abstentionism, recognize that citizenship is indeed premised on common moral values, and actively promote those civic virtues that underpin citizenship. That these 'common values' or 'civic virtues' might encapsulate the moral perspectives of some groups but not others does not figure very prominently in this.

The communitarian strand of civic republicanism is also less sensitive than it should be to relationships of domination and hierarchy within existing communities. It directs its critical energy against the rampant individualism that encourages us to focus on rights to the exclusion of duties, or the freedoms to do as we will in our private lives to the exclusion of civic engagement. Most incensed by a political culture that promotes the free agency of autonomous and isolated individuals, it often ignores equally compelling criticism of the coercions practised by communities. Yet communities have their undoubted downside. Even if we set aside the more overtly inegalitarian cases where the young are subordinated to the old or women to men, communities operate by imposing constraints on the kinds of thing 'we' do or the kinds of thing 'we' think. To be a member is to acknowledge these constraints. Those who challenge them too decisively soon find themselves rank outsiders.

It is clear enough that no society can survive on the basis of market relations alone; some additional cement is always required to secure diverse individuals in a network of sustainable relationships. Sometimes it is the family that does this job, sometimes the church, sometimes a more amorphous public opinion mobilized through associations in civil society. Mass political parties did their bit through much of the twentieth century, and even the stark left–right antagonisms on which such parties were based could be said to have contributed a solidaristic counter-weight to the fragmentations of market society. But mass parties now seem rather empty shells, the family is widely regarded as in crisis (the hierarchical family is undoubtedly so), and despite the extraordinary influence of religion on political life in the USA, the church (particularly not 'the' church) can no longer present itself as the unquestioned repository of moral values. The communitarian turn in political theory is in large part a response to this sense of impending crisis. Faced with a more naked individualism than was ever anticipated by classical liberalism, communitarian thinkers have looked to the 'community' as the source of shared values and social cohesion.

The danger in this is that it so often invokes an undifferentiated and unified community. In my view, the resuscitation of dying forms of communal solidarity is neither possible nor desirable. People are not going to return to unquestioned loyalties of family or religion or locality, and given the hierarchical nature of most traditional forms of community, their recalcitrance is to be encouraged rather than quashed. Nor are they going to return to the solidarities of class that were celebrated through generations of socialist politics. The class structure that underpinned this solidarity has decisively altered, and the brotherhood that was so insistently masculine has little resonance in the modern world. Better, by far, to see solidarities as forged out of alliances between people who are different, or community as constructed in an explicitly political realm. It is 'constructed' that is the key word here, implying a process based on different constitutive elements that may continue to be in tension. The more communitarian version of civic republicanism is not sufficiently attuned to this.

One of the other criticisms levelled at civic republicanism (in both communitarian and more political versions) is that it promotes an ideal of citizenship as transcendence: citizens leaving behind their egotistical interests and partial preoccupations to achieve the higher unities of the public sphere. Modern-day republicans do not, on the whole, set much store by ideas of 'a' common good, and nearly all of them distance themselves from what are felt to be pre-modern notions of an undifferentiated homogeneous citizenry.[15] They none the less stress the importance of a politics that can aim at (even if it does not reach) shared visions, and they often present this in opposition to private needs and concerns. Citizens should be focusing on what they have in common rather than on what makes them different. They should be aiming at the impartial promotion of public good, not the partial promotion of private concerns.

In her criticism of this, Iris Young argues that the impartial general perspective is a myth, and that in 'a society where some groups are privileged while others are oppressed, insisting that as citizens persons should leave behind their particular affiliations and experiences to adopt a general point of view serves only to reinforce the privilege'.[16] What is at issue here is not whether people should feel entitled to favour their own group to the exclusion of everyone else's: partiality, in this sense, is as abhorrent to Young as to the most high-minded of civic republicans. The question, rather, is whether calling on people to set their own particular affiliations to one side is the route to a more just democracy. When a disabled person, for example, is asked to give judgement on some project for public spending, should she be thinking about what will be useful to society as a whole or just what will help people with her own disability? If the disability is shared by a tiny number of people, should she bracket it out, put it to one side, think only about what will benefit the overwhelming majority? Or since she too is part of the society (in however tiny a fraction), should she point out that the new building will be inaccessible to people in wheelchairs or the new library useless to people who are blind?

On examples like this, most people will probably say she should draw on her own knowledge and experiences, and that it is only through interventions such as hers that societies have learnt to make their public projects more genuinely accessible to all. We might be less sympathetic, however, to childless people who refuse to pay any more for public education, or wealthy people who refuse to contribute any more to the welfare state. In these instances, we are more likely to find the intrusion of private experience a problem, to say that people should be more public-spirited and put their own private gains to one side. In the context of an unequal society, the injunction on particularity sometimes works against the less privileged and sometimes works in their favour. It can make it harder for members of disadvantaged groups to draw attention to their specific needs or oppressions (we don't make policies just for your bunch, we have to address wider concerns), but it can also make it easier to challenge those who want to opt out of public responsibilities because they do not personally benefit from these. Young tends to stress the first point to the exclusion of the second. This is because her analysis of structural inequalities suggests to her that appeals to impartiality set oppressed groups at a particular disadvantage.

She makes the point that we test out whether claims are merely self-interested by requiring people to confront others making different kinds of claim, and that it is through arguing with those who have different experiences and priorities that we are best able to establish whether our own proposals are just. Trying to pre-empt this by limiting people to what they can reasonably present as being in the general interest makes it more likely that they will restrict themselves to what is already in the public domain. This makes it more likely that they will reproduce a current consensus. I am often struck by the self-censorship people operate when formulating their own policy preferences, as if they have to take all the objections on board even before presenting their own point of view. If others are less self-denying, this skews the outcome in their favour; while if everyone decides to tone down his or her claims, this seriously curtails the range of debate. Though Jürgen Habermas has been criticized for an excessive attachment to universal and impartial reason, he makes a similar point when he observes that a premature leap into impartiality would exclude controversial ethical questions, unnecessarily delimit the public from the private, and 'at least implicitly prejudice the agenda in favour of an inherited background of settled traditions'.[17] We need the vitality of what Habermas calls 'wild' or 'anarchic' opinion-formation in order to counter the exclusionary effects of unequally distributed power. A democracy that tries to limit in advance what can or cannot be said will not deal adequately with the political consequences of social inequality. This remains the case even when the intentions are of the best, as when civic republicans seek to exclude private interest from political affairs.

Civic republicanism tends to be rather weak on structural power relations, employing categories of virtue or civic participation to counter the power of interest, but not looking carefully enough at the ways these interests are produced and reproduced. It sometimes gives the impression that we can solve our problems by exhorting one another to behave in a more public-spirited way, with no further reference to the conditions that have made us behave so differently. 'Its categories serve to obscure questions of power and authority and to sever political activity from specific localities, thereby producing an abstract category "participation", which can be enlarged or attenuated, depending on research needs.' In Sheldon Wolin's view, this 'has the effect of muting the tensions between republicanism, with its strong historical attraction to elitism, and democracy, with its irreducibly populist strain'.[18]

Freedom as non-domination

In a very different retrieval of the republican tradition, Philip Pettit argues that the defining core lies less in ideals of active political participation or the pursuit of common interest, and more in the notion of freedom as non-domination.[19] On this reading, the revival of republicanism is less likely to sever connections between 'good' politics and structural inequalities. Though he approaches this through a critique of arbitrary rule rather than a critique of inequality *per se*, Pettit also provides some additional weight to my argument about the relationship between political and economic equality. To be exposed to the arbitrary will of another is the greatest evil in the republican canon: the exposure to tyrannical and unchecked rulers; but also to the dominance of employers over workers or the dominance of husbands over wives. Wherever one party has the capacity to interfere on an arbitrary basis in the choices another party is in a position to make, we are looking at an example of dominance. Republicanism does not require us to eliminate income differentials between employers and workers, but it certainly implies measures to eliminate capricious powers of hiring and firing, and it would secure the right to collective action through which workers can defend themselves. Republicanism also does not seem to require the strict equality in the division of labour I have argued for between women and men. It does, however, imply intervention to eliminate those cultural, legal, and institutional pressures that conspire to keep women in a condition akin to slavery and still subject to the domination of men.

The idea that domination is distinct from economic inequality has been a recurrent theme in the history of egalitarian politics. One frequent argument from nineteenth-century feminism was that middle-class women were more confined, disparaged and oppressed than poorer women who at least had the dignity of employment: as one leading British suffragist put this, 'A great lady or a factory woman are independent persons – personages – the women of the middle classes are nobodies, and if they act for themselves they lose caste!'[20] The economic impoverishment of women from the middle classes was also a recurrent theme (their terrible vulnerability in a world that expected them to find an income through marriage and thwarted their attempts to enter the labour market for themselves), but the importance attached to women's independence, autonomy, and self-respect generated an understanding of inequality that went well beyond statistics on poverty or hours and conditions of work. Feminists have always been clear that money is not everything, and this is a theme that reappeared in the 1960s with Betty Friedan's analysis of the suburban housewife's malaise. A woman surrounded by the latest in kitchen gadgets can have less sense of her own worth than another who has to struggle for her subsistence; relationships of domination can persist even when material conditions are relatively secure.

Though he steers clear of any strong association between economic and political equality, Pettit endorses a version of republicanism that includes a robust social radicalism: always troubled by any evidence of domination; always prepared to take measures to deal with this. Freedom conceived as non-interference (the more traditionally liberal understanding) makes people wary of state intervention. We get locked into a defence of individual rights and freedoms, and intuitively distrust proposals that seek to make the 'formal' rights more effective if these depend on heavy interference by the state. When freedom is conceived, by contrast, as non-domination, 'we are going to look more fondly on state interference'.[21] So long as the state is bound by constraints that make its interference non-arbitrary (this depends in turn on whether the democracy is inclusive, deliberative and always open to popular contestation), the fact that it interferes is no great objection. If it interferes to reduce domination, this is regarded as a definite plus.

Other versions of republicanism have been more exercised by the way private interest can threaten public good. Because of this, they have been more inclined to see the comparative obsessions of equality (does he have more than I?) as destructive of political life. A republicanism that makes freedom from domination the central category is going to be more hospitable to social radicalism, and more prepared to look beyond the conventionally political sphere to address an array of potentially oppressive relationships in employment or the family. But even this most promising version fails to get to grips with the tension between political equality/economic inequality that lies at the heart of this book. First, inequalities will matter only in so far as they create a direct relationship of domination and subordination: this focuses attention on inequalities that give power *over* others, leaving to one side those additional inequalities that may just give some people more than the rest. Secondly, domination is conceived as exposure to an arbitrary or capricious will; this encourages us to take issue with 'bad' employers but has little to say against those who set up works councils or manage to make fully transparent their own principles and procedures. Inequalities that are systemic drop out of the picture.

Deliberative democracy

In the related literature that has sprung up around notions of deliberative democracy there is also a tension between different variants, with some more hospitable to economic equality than others. All exponents of deliberative democracy make some stab in the direction of 'free and equal access'. They argue that political decisions should emerge out of the unconstrained deliberation of all those likely to be affected,[22] and they see the legitimacy of these decisions as seriously compromised if it turns out that certain people were being excluded from the debate. Deliberative democrats vary, however, in the attention they give to guaranteeing this freedom of access – and all too often, the 'free and equal' condition becomes notional rather than real. They also vary in their attitude to expressions of economic interest. Some regard deliberation as a means of escaping the unhealthy intrusion of interest into politics, and look to it to promote a more altruistic pursuit of the common good. Others argue that deliberation matters precisely because people do have different identities, perspectives and interests, and that these have to be embraced within the process of discussion rather than ruled out in advance.

So what do I mean by deliberative democracy? The idea that democracy is about deliberation is not a new one. People have always discussed things before reaching a decision and deliberated over the issues at hand. Until relatively recently, the value attached to deliberation tended to be in inverse proportion to the value attached to popular control. When Edmund Burke warned his Bristol constituents that they should not expect him to act just as their mouthpiece, he was stressing the importance of deliberation in a legislative assembly. They should elect him to deliberate, to employ his own judgement in working out their 'real' interests, and not to promote whatever causes they held dear. In this version, the value attached to deliberation has looked rather elitist, an insistence on the discretionary powers of the legislative body, and a refusal to be bound by the voters' concerns.

The radical retrieval of deliberation has developed from two directions: first a critique of the interest-aggregation model of democracy that turns politics into an inglorious market; second, a recognition of pluralism and difference as built into the framework of contemporary life. The first is very much a reaction to the shallowness of liberal democracy – what Benjamin Barber describes as a 'thin' democracy[23] – that takes it as given that people have conflicting interests and preferences and tries only to keep the competition in check. One crucial argument here is that what we conceive of as our preferences and interests changes when we discuss it with others. You may consider abortion immoral, I may be equally convinced it is immoral to force a woman to continue a pregnancy against her will, but some at least of our disagreement may come from not having considered the other's arguments or not having realized certain salient facts.

A decision-making model that simply asks us to vote on the issue allows no space for reconsidering our own point of view. A deliberative model, by contrast, requires people to put forward arguments: to defend a case, not just cast a secret vote. This should filter out illegitimate appeals based only on self-interest, but it also means that all of us may change. The great value of discussion and argument is that it can lead people to modify their initial positions, making possible, as Jane Mansbridge puts it, 'solutions that were impossible before the process began'.[24]

The second point is that the recognition of pluralism and difference has turned theorists away from the authoritative foundations on which people might hope to ground their political or moral views and towards a more political interpretation of the processes through which different belief-systems or perspectives are accommodated. Deliberative democracy is premised on the notion that the truth arrives, if at all, from a free and fair interchange between diverse opinions and perspectives. All of us have reason to doubt our own initial intuitions or convictions, and it is only in the process of arguing for these with people of very different persuasions that we can hope to arrive at a just conclusion. The process then becomes the guarantee. We cannot expect to arrive at the right conclusions through a private interrogation in which we dig deeper into our own personal belief-systems, or a Hobbesian deduction that conceives of moral and political beliefs on an analogy with the principles of geometry. Nor can we imagine that the truths are simply located in the shared traditions of our society, as some of the deeper communitarians would have us believe. The consensus will be generated through politics not society, and it is the quality of the democracy that will guarantee the quality of the results.

The first part of the argument refuses to treat politics on the model of the market economy, and rejects the huckstering and bargaining associated with this. This is often posed as a criticism of contemporary party politics, which is widely regarded as evacuating the arena of informed debate to compete for voter support on the basis of crudely defined (often personality-driven) appeals. More fundamentally, it takes issue with an interest-driven conception of politics that assumes an array of individuals and pressure groups all jostling for resources and attention, and regards democracy as just a protective mechanism to guard against the dominance of any one group. In contrast to this, deliberative democracy puts a premium on refined and reflective preferences that would be ' *"fact-regarding"* (as opposed to igno-rant or doctrinaire), *"future-regarding"* (as opposed to myopic) and *"other-regarding"* (as opposed to selfish)'.[25] The radicalism in this is relatively easy to spot. Instead of the short-termism encouraged by capitalist production, we might then be better equipped to address long-term environmental issues. And instead of the selfishness engendered by a competitive market economy, we might find ourselves deciding things on the basis of what is just.

The second part goes a long way towards meeting the concerns of those who view majoritarian politics as imposing one group's norms on all others, and this has contributed to a strong associ-ation between deliberative democracy and multicultural cit-izenship. Where a rights-based understanding of democracy might draw up an *a priori* list of fundamental rights, deliberative democrats are more likely to stress the importance of intercul-tural dialogue in formulating central principles. This recognizes the essential contestability of even the most dominant conven-tions and opens up space for a more resolutely multicultural approach. Similarly, where a votes-driven understanding of democracy would simply aggregate existing preferences, the deliberative model encourages participants in dialogue to recog-nize when their initial judgements were formed out of ignorance or prejudice. In the first case, progressives keep their fingers crossed and hope the xenophobic right fails to win enough votes; in the second case, racism is more directly confronted and some of it may then dissolve. Deliberative models of democracy look to the transformative effects of discussion in deepening our understanding of political choices, and alerting us to the legiti-macy of other people's claims. It is hardly surprising that this has been presented as peculiarly appropriate to societies that are multicultural and/or contain significant ethnic minorities.[26]

Procedures and conditions

With all these compelling strengths, deliberative democracy is not very good on questions of equality. The first point is that writers within this school often fail to address the conditions for free and equal access carefully enough. They have certainly come up with a number of imaginative suggestions that could help promote informed and considered judgement among a wider range of citizens: the use, for example, of deliberative opinion polls that would allow ordinary voters to explore issues directly with candidates before elections;[27] or the creation of socially representative 'citizens' juries' to make recommendations between a range of policy alternatives. (This last has been the subject of experimentation by some local authorities in Britain.) Such initiatives do not draw their participants from the usual political elite, and because they typically operate through a process of random sampling – in much the same way as legal juries are formed – they can reasonably claim to be more fully representative of a diversity of citizens. Precisely because of this, however, they are almost always conceived as consultative bodies. A citizens' jury does not wield active power.

The idea that a more deliberative democracy generates more just decisions depends crucially on the assumption that all voices are being fairly heard. Failing serious efforts to deliver this equality, deliberative models of democracy become little more than a pious attachment to informed over ill-informed decisions, or a belief in the power of discussion as making possible solutions that were impossible before. We know all this just from our daily experience in social encounters; we know we find out things through discussion; we know that talking things over helps. The extra claim attached to political deliberation – the belief that the outcomes will then be more just – depends on whether all voices are indeed being heard. This can only mean, in my view, that a coherent programme for deliberative democracy has to deal with the social composition of the people making the final decisions. This is not adequately dealt with by the use of 'focus groups' or 'citizens' juries' to test out popular reaction to proposed policies. It means that decision-making assemblies themselves (including our legislative assemblies) have to be opened up to all relevant groups.

Ways of ensuring this might range from a use of gender quotas to ensure parity between women and men, a use of proportional electoral systems to promote better representation for people from racial and ethnic minorities, to something like the group representation proposals outlined by Iris Young. This is the point, however, at which too many advocates of deliberative democracy back away. Part of the dream of deliberation is that it will diminish the 'groupiness' that locks people into their own group's interests and concerns: how can this be made compatible with measures that seek to secure the representation of all relevant groups? Even bearing in mind the distinction I made earlier between representing a 'group' and representing those with a shared group characteristic, measures for guaranteed representation inevitably draw attention to group difference and division, to the fact that workers have different interests from employers, women from men, black people from white, ethnic minorities from ethnic majorities. In doing so, they not only argue for special initiatives to counter persistent under-representation. They also measure the success of these initiatives by whether the new representatives speak from the experiences of their group. If the election of more women MPs, for example, does not raise the profile of women's interests and concerns, it will be regarded as a failure by many of those who promoted it. The whole point was to make a difference, and that depends on treating women as in some sense a distinct social group.

The sticking point for many advocates of deliberative democracy is that this edges too close to a politics based on interest, and it was the critique of that politics that first started them on their route. There are important exceptions to this trend: Iris Young, most notably;[28] to a lesser extent also Cass Sunstein, who argues that group representation is incompatible with the deeper aims of deliberation if it is conceived just as a way of ensuring that each group gets 'a piece of the action', but becomes far more acceptable if its function is to prevent the false appearance of a common set of interests and promote one more genuinely inclusive.[29] But even this concession can leave the requirement for equitable representation dependent on whether it manages to promote 'good' deliberation. Discussing the case for compensatory group representation, Amy Gutmann and Dennis Thompson argue that this can only be justified if it 'encourages more representatives to pay more attention to the voices of neglected citizens, fosters co-operation between representatives of these citizens and representatives of other citizens, and stimulates all representatives to give reasons and invoke moral principles that cut across racial and group divisions'.[30] The implication is that if it fails to have these effects – if it ends up only as a way of including previously marginalized groups – it is not to be encouraged. The requirement for equality is then subordinated to the critique of interest-group politics, and the second always trumps the first. The resulting ambivalence towards equality contributes to a certain airiness in the literature on deliberative democracy, a tendency to specify the conditions and then forget about whether these match up to any given reality.

The second point is that the focus on deliberation as a means of resolving political dilemmas inadvertently shifts attention from those that arise out of conflicts of interest to those that reflect failures of communication. A deliberative approach to problem solving is said to encourage open-mindedness, a willingness to listen to others, and a 'civic magnanimity'[31] that recognizes the moral seriousness even of those with whom we most profoundly disagree. All this is valuable advice for anyone trying to set up healthy conditions for debate: we do not get very far when people simply shout at one another, impugn the other side's credentials, or refuse to consider an alternative point of view. And where disagreements turn out to be based on ignorance and prejudice, these conditions of mutual respect can prove immensely productive. Most of us harbour certain prejudices based on the way people dress or speak: a presumption, perhaps, that the scruffily dressed youth in dreadlocks will have nothing worth saying except on some topics relating to music, or that the man in the turban will be a religious fundamentalist, or the woman with the cut-glass accent a caricature of her class. Most of us also harbour what we regard as more legitimate pre-judgements based on a long process of opinion formation: a distrust, perhaps, of arguments that turn on economic efficiency or arguments that resort to divine will. Retaining a permanent state of openness can seem rather time-wasting, particularly if we feel we have established good grounds for pre-judgements. But both types of pre-judgement may be modified in subsequent discussion, and a willingness to engage with the appropriate seriousness often has positive effects.

The effects are most marked, however, where disagreements are rooted in a previous failure to hear. Some of the problems that arise in societies that are multi-ethnic or multicultural fit well enough into this pattern: an inability to register what others are saying; a subsequent release from this disabling impasse when participants adopt a more open-minded approach. But while the frequent association with multiculturalism can be viewed as one of the strengths of the deliberative tradition, it also highlights some of the weaknesses. It often seems that discussions of multiculturalism have supplanted earlier discussions of racism, and that the previous emphasis on starker inequalities in housing, education or employment has given way to a preoccupation with cultural or doctrinal difference. In much of the European debate about multicultural citizenship, the paradigmatic problem is now the accommodation of Muslim minorities. These are notoriously exposed to demonization as an incomprehensible 'other', and failures in communication or recognition rank high in the 'problem' they supposedly pose. A politics that promotes more sustained intercultural dialogue looks particularly appropriate to this context, for it directly addresses issues of recognition. It may have less obvious purchase where what is at issue is the distribution of economic or social resources between majority and minority groups.   .

Not all problems are amenable to resolution through discussion, for some do take the form of a starker zero-sum game. If wages are to rise, profits must fall. If women are to be equal to men, men must lose some of their present advantages. If black South Africans are to have more land, white South Africans must have less. Conditions of reasonable discussion may generate a consensus in favour of redistribution. It may be possible to convince those who lose out that their current privileges are illegitimate. It may even be possible to convince them that they can live more happily under more just conditions and that the quality of their lives will improve. If the argument fails, however, we are still left with a conflict of interests. Jane Mansbridge makes the point that models of democracy geared towards mutual understanding and consensus do not work so well when there is conflict over principles of fair distribution, and that we may need 'institutions based primarily on self-interest as well as those based on altruism'.[32] She also notes that deliberation can serve as a mask for domination, and that when deliberative theorists rule self-interest out of politics, they seem to be forgetting relations of power.

One of the dangers in deliberative models is that criticizing the role of interest in politics can bear more harshly on the dispossessed than on the advantaged. If the value attached to deliberation makes it harder for such groups to talk the language of interests, this can end up confirming the status quo. The related danger is that those calling for what will be regarded as 'extreme' solutions will find it harder to make their interventions in the recommended style. People often find themselves in situations where they cannot produce the arguments that will back up what they intuitively believe to be right. Sometimes this is because there simply are no plausible arguments, in which case one might say they are rightly silenced. But sometimes it is because the arguments they would like to offer just seem too off the wall, too much at odds with the prevailing consensus for anyone to put them forward and still appear sane. Germaine Greer once said that women's liberation would not happen 'unless individual women agree to be outcasts, eccentrics, perverts, and whatever the powers-that-be choose to call them'.[33] Fortunately for the rest of us, enough individual women agreed to take on the mantle of insanity (and were helped in this by the fact that there were a lot of them around). The 'reasonable' face of feminism has always derived part of its energy from the wilder activities of its 'radical' fringe, as when those crazy women breaking windows and chaining themselves to railings gave new prominence to the law-abiding suffragist campaigns. In the calmer reaches of deliberative democracy, excess and extremism have no place. Yet without these, there would be less chance of change.

One way of thinking of this is to say that democracies need advocates as well as deliberators: they need the intransigent narrowness of those who refuse to budge from their initial positions as well as the more comprehensive vision that comes with taking on board opposing positions and adjusting to what other people have said. The process in which fiery advocates get transformed into reasonable deliberators is familiar enough to any observer of contemporary politics. It is often described as co-option and sometimes as betrayal. One would hardly want to defend a vision of politics in which people never listened to their opponents, never revised their opinions, never submitted to the power of the better argument. But the good deliberator is not necessarily the best of advocates, for the more skilled we become in entering into other people's positions or adapting our arguments to what they will find persuasive, the more likely it is that we will detach ourselves from the community whose interests we initially shared. In societies where there are structural inequalities of power, the resulting consensus may close down important options.

It would be wrong to suggest that those writing about deliberative democracy fail to notice the inequalities of contemporary society: wrong not only because some writers within this tradition (most notably, Iris Young) are centrally concerned with these inequalities, but also because one of the hopes attached to deliberation is that it will make justice the key player in political debate. At its best, an interest-aggregation model of democracy can only help those who form the numerical majority. At its worst, it won't even help these, for even majorities can be persuaded to vote for policies that go against their interests, and quite often do so when they are convinced there are no alternatives around. The hope attached to deliberation is that it filters out arguments based on self-interest and replaces them by arguments based on justice instead. This is said to be far more promising as a way of dealing with racial injustice, for in detaching the power of the argument from the weight of the numbers, it opens up the possibility that groups forming a numerical minority might win the others to their side.[34]

It has also been said to be more promising as a way of dealing with poverty, for once justice begins to shape the discussion, we are more likely to consider poverty unjust. The interest-aggregation model tends to take preferences as fixed and given. One of the problems with this is that preferences are always formed in relation to what has become a social norm. If we have come to think that certain claims are legitimate (perhaps because of the successes of some earlier political movement, or of what is now enshrined in our country's laws), then we are more likely to press them. Failing that, we tend to put up with our current conditions. We do not like to live in a state of permanent resentment, so we adjust our expectations downwards in order to survive and remain sane. The result is that people often adapt themselves to 'undue limitations in available opportunities or to unjust background conditions':[35] it is because of this, one might suggest, that universal suffrage has had less of an effect on the distribution of property than its opponents once feared. If we take the preferences expressed through the vote as the final word on what governments should do, we may be condemning large sections of the community (in this case, it might even be a majority) to persistently unjust conditions. A more deliberative process of policy formation could reopen those closed doors.

To this extent, the 'calling back to politics' implied in the literature on republicanism and deliberation could promote a stronger social radicalism that begins to address inequalities in income and power. The point I have stressed is that failing sustained efforts to deliver on political equality – and by implication, sustained initiatives on economic equality – this remains a promissory note. The value attached to deliberation depends on whether 'all those affected' really are included and involved; all too often, the critique of interest-group politics acts to block serious initiatives on this. If deliberation is to mean something other than what Edmund Burke meant by it – something more, that is, than a rejection of binding mandates, or a celebration of the legislators' discretionary powers – it has to be combined with measures that guarantee more inclusive decision-making assemblies. Its credibility depends on whether there really is free and equal access to decision-making arenas, and whether all those possibly affected by the decisions really do get their chance to agree. It depends on a far more substantive political equality than we currently enjoy. That, in turn, depends on more substantive economic equality.

6
Equal Yet Unequal?

Not so long ago, it was commonplace to scorn easy protestations of equality in the context of an unequal world. How could anyone seriously claim that rich and poor enjoyed the same political status, or that money was irrelevant to the exercise of civil and political rights? How could anyone think that giving women the equal right to vote made the two sexes equal, when men never lifted a finger to help with the housework and women were laughed out of court if they attempted 'masculine' jobs? The gap between formal and real, 'merely' political and substantive equality, was evident enough to anyone who cared to see. If claims to equality were to acquire any deeper significance, they would have to be allied to major programmes of social and economic change.

For a variety of (good and bad) reasons, proclamations of equality in the midst of inequality have come to seem far less paradoxical today. Among the good reasons is the recognition that civil and political rights matter, and that a society based on universal suffrage, popularly contested elections, and equality before the law is superior to one that dispenses with these equalities even when its economic arrangements leave much to be desired. Political equality is no small achievement, and people still risk their lives struggling for 'merely' political rights. 'In the repression and frozen privation of 1795, the cry is not for "Bread", but for "Bread and the Constitution of 1793".'[1] What was true for the French Revolution continues true to the present day, though knowledge of this has occasionally faltered.

Political equality matters even if undermined by economic inequality. It matters as a statement of intent and a standard against which to measure future achievements. More straightforwardly, it matters because it already delivers something even when that something is not so grand as it promised to be. A society that recognizes all adults as political equals recognizes their equal right to vote and stand for election; within certain limits set by political order, it also recognizes the equal legitimacy of each citizen's point of view. The first of these will not equalize their political influence, but it does mean that each citizen carries the same weight in the moment of casting a vote and that none can be rejected without reason in the selection of candidates for office. (You can be rejected without what you regard as *good* reason, but it still matters that reasons have to be given.) The second does not guarantee equality of respect, but does mean that the most frowned-upon of opinions will still be tolerated if they cannot be shown to do anyone any harm. These achievements are not to be dismissed as 'merely' political.

Appreciation of the more basic rights and equalities tends to be strongest among those still denied them (familiarity breeds complacency, if not always contempt), and the rather shame-faced recognition of this fact is part of what has shifted opinion in the more established democracies. Critics of liberal democracy have sometimes suggested that there is not much to choose between one-party and multi-party systems, or that there is only a sliver of difference between civilian and military regimes, neither of which allows for substantive popular control. Such arguments usually appear less persuasive to those still living under military or one-party rule. Disparagement of voting rights as fooling people into thinking they are equal has also had less resonance among groups not yet granted the rights of citizenship or prevented from registering to vote. An equality that leaves other inequalities untouched can still be vitally important; this is more widely accepted among social critics than it was in the 1960s or 1970s.

It hardly needs saying that this change of heart took place during the waxing of liberalism and waning of socialism, a process that simultaneously threw into relief the importance of political rights and equalities and the difficulties of achieving fundamental economic change. I am not sure whether to put this into the category of good or bad reasons for changing one's views on the relationship between political and economic equality: good, I suppose, if it stops people embarking on poorly thought-out and harshly imposed programmes of economic transformation; bad if it encourages them to put up with whatever economic inequalities happen to emerge. Countries still vary significantly in their internal distribution of income and wealth, their social provision for education and health, and the tax rates they impose; even within the broad framework of market society and capitalist production, there is considerable scope for reducing economic inequality. It may be utopian to talk of eliminating all inequalities. It is not utopian to say economic inequalities can be significantly reduced.

The decoupling of political from economic equality arises, in part, from the belief that it is easier to act on the first than the second. I have suggested that it also arises from a recognition that political equality is less advanced in the established democracies than previous generations thought it to be, and that there is a great deal of unfinished business in working out what it means to treat citizens as equals. I have referred to more straightforward examples of this, like the current attack on principles of hereditary privilege in the British House of Lords. I have discussed (at somewhat greater length) more controversial examples, like the growing conviction that political equality remains incomplete until there is a more equitable distribution of elected positions between black and white, women and men, and that procedures should be put in place to break existing monopolies. In earlier discussions, discrepancies between statement and reality – between saying all citizens have the same political rights regardless of sex or the colour of their skin, and then finding that those elected are typically male and white – might have been taken as proving the inadequacy of 'merely' political equality. Nowadays, it is more commonly taken as evidence that political equality is not yet in place.

In this, as in other examples discussed through the book, the meaning of political equality has been revisited, and the idea that citizens already enjoy their equal civil and political rights has been held up to closer scrutiny. Where earlier generations sometimes gave the impression that the battle for civil and political rights was over and that all remaining activity would take place in the economic realm, current thinking stresses the very patchy nature of citizenship, particularly for women and those in an ethnic or racial minority. This does not mean people have retreated from grand projects of economic equalization to content themselves with their meagre political rights. A more accurate description is that much of the energy that used to go into promoting economic equality now goes into deepening and extending equalities in the political sphere.

A major part of this, I have argued, is the reworking of equality to address questions of difference. Wry comments about rich and poor being equally entitled to the protection of the law to defend their private property, or equally entitled to sleep out on the streets at night, also alert us to the emptiness in seeing equality as a matter of treating everyone the same. But examples derived from differences in income or wealth play on the unequal impact of same treatment when applied to people in unequal conditions, suggesting that it may be necessary to treat people differently (perhaps give more to the poor rather than the same as is given to the rich) in order to produce a similar outcome. This does not take issue with sameness as an objective, only with foolish notions that this objective could be achieved by ignoring self-evident inequalities.

Examples derived from differences in culture, religion, ethnicity – to a lesser extent, gender or race – are more likely to query the desirability of sameness. The argument that same treatment, regardless of differences of sex or race, is not always the best route to equality stays reasonably close to the argument that treating rich and poor the same only confirms their inequality. The idea that equal citizenship should not be made to depend on women proving themselves the same as men more explicitly queries the value of sameness. So, too, does the argument that refusing to sanction any differences of treatment for minority cultural groups can unfairly impose majority norms on minority groups; or that refusing to accommodate indigenous peoples in their efforts to sustain distinct legal and political traditions can end up as forced assimilation. When most countries are culturally, linguistically and ethnically diverse – when minorities and majorities 'increasingly clash over such issues as language rights, regional autonomy, political representation, education curriculum, land claims, immigration and naturalization policy, even national symbols'[2] – the idea that equal citizenship involves assimilating minorities into whatever happen to be the majority's norms seems patently unfair. It should not be necessary for people to make themselves the same as the others in order to qualify for equal respect.

Democracies have to be able to recognize their citizens as equal though different: this is one of the points I have laboured. It is a confusion of categories, however, to slide from this to saying people can be equal yet unequal. In the history of gender relations, there was a long tradition of presenting women as men's superiors: often enough, not just equal and different but different and superior, with the women represented as more refined, more sensitive, more moral than the men. (It was usually the men who said this: Mary Wollstonecraft trashed the idea.) Feminists became skilled in recognizing such protestations of respect for what they were, and many of them came to dislike the very sound of 'equal but different'. Others did see the sexes as different, but doubted the intentions of those who employed this difference to justify unequal treatment in employment or education or law. The key question has always been whether it makes sense to talk of equality of respect between groups whose material conditions are so markedly different. Equality might not mean sameness, but can it be compatible with such an extra-ordinary imbalance in income, life-chances and power?

Recent discourses of difference have, to some extent, muddied the waters around equality by making convergence in material conditions seem too much of an assimilationist goal. In the case of feminism, there is a line of argument that views claims to employment equality as overly tarnished by images of women making themselves 'equal' by turning themselves into facsimiles of men, and prefers to insist on the distinctive values associated with mothering and the many reasons why women might choose to stay at home with their children rather than pursuing high-paid careers. This is fine as a critique of any version of feminism that treated children as an obstruction, or saw sexual equality as women assimilating themselves to the life-patterns of men. It is less compelling as a critique of convergence, where the main concern has been to enable both women and men to change the patterns of their lives.

Important as it is, the emphasis on difference risks turning equality into a pure act of will: people *will* be regarded as equals, despite, even sometimes because of, the differences in their lives. There are cases where the struggle for equality does centre on changing attitudes or cultural symbols: Nancy Fraser offers the example of homophobia, which will be fully overcome (along with its attendant economic injustices) only when the status order that values heterosexuals over homosexuals has changed. My working assumption is still that most struggles for equality will depend on some modification in economic conditions: to put this starkly, that aboriginals in Australia need hospitals as well as recognition, that Muslim minorities in Europe need better schools as well as Islamic ones, and that women everywhere need the right to reclaim paid employment after maternity leave as well as to be valued for their activities as mothers. Some, at least, of the changes will be about reducing group differences in order to reduce inequalities.

Hannah Arendt once described political equality as 'an equality of unequals who stand in need of being "equalized" in certain respects and for certain purposes'.[3] It then arises only when people are not equal and would hardly be coherent if everyone were already the same. At one level, Arendt's observation must be correct. If 'political equality' is to mean anything distinct from unqualified 'equality' – if there is to be any point in talking of a specifically *political* equality – it must refer in some way to inequality. Why do people insist that they are politically equal? Because in some other respect, they are not regarded as equal: maybe in respect to something you take more seriously than I do, like my lack of connections in high places; maybe in respect to something we both recognize as significant, like the discrepancy in our incomes; maybe in respect to something that bothers me more than you, like my ignorance of nuclear physics? Claims to political equality always carry a background echo of something that makes this equality surprising. We are equals despite various significant inequalities; we are political, even if not total, equals.

If we accept that this is part of what is implied by political equality, we can hardly see it as contradicted by *any* evidence of inequality in other aspects of our lives. The question, rather, is whether democracies can 'equalize unequals' through a pure act of proclamation (what might be described as the town-crier theory of equality), or have to establish certain conditions. I have argued that there are indeed conditions, and that it is never enough just to proclaim that citizens must have 'free and equal access' to political life. So long as large sections of the citizenry are constrained in the exercise of their political rights by lack of money, education, contacts, or time, declarations of basic equality will always ring rather hollow. Formal rights to participate in politics always raise questions about what makes these rights effective. The answers to these questions will include strong measures to equalize educational and employment opportunities and to sustain social mobility throughout people's lives; they will also include remedial measures (such as gender quotas) to counteract what would otherwise be the 'natural' effects of an existing distribution of occupation or income.[4]

Inequalities in political access disturb the complacent surface of democratic life, but even more telling, in my view, is the difficulty of ensuring equality of status when people are so markedly unequal in their material conditions. When the case for greater economic equality is made to turn exclusively on whether individuals have the effective right to participate in politics, it turns on a patronizing – and in its starker formulations, unconvincing – thesis about the rich being politically energetic and the poor politically inert. This does not fit too well with the history of political activism, but it also loads political life with more importance than it can bear. If the only reason for redistributing income and wealth is that this will allow me to participate more fully in politics, I might well decline the favour: I might feel my life is busy enough already without having to take up politics as well. Understood in the narrower sense of equality in political participation and influence, political equality is not a strong enough basis on which to build arguments for economic reform. It is when we take it as a deeper claim about holding all citizens in equal regard that the connections become more compelling.

Political equality, in this deeper sense, has become one of the defining beliefs of the current age – in a way that makes a nonsense of unqualified assertions about people giving up on egalitarian ideals. In my perception, people now care more rather than less about equality. They are more insistent on their standing as equals (what makes him think he is better than I? what makes her think she can tell me what to do?), less prepared to accept a subordinate position or believe everything the authorities say. Faced with evidence that political influence is distributed according to wealth or family connections, many budding egalitarians may still shrug their shoulders: who, in the end, cares? But faced with evidence that one kind of person is regarded as of less account than some other – that office workers are considered of less account than executives, plumbers of less account than doctors, or women of less account than men – the most accommodating of individuals is likely to register a complaint. Taken in this broader sense, this is a time of greater egalitarianism, not less.

Because there *is* a relationship between social standing and material conditions, certain things then follow about the way democracies have to organize their economic affairs. A society that condones excesses of poverty in the midst of wealth, or arbitrarily rewards one skill with one hundred times the wages of another, is not recognizing its citizens as of equal human worth. On the contrary, it is making it harder than ever for the members of that society to keep up their pretence that they consider their fellow citizens their equals. There are always some individuals capable of that act of imagination that discards social and economic stereotypes and looks through differences in income, experience, or wealth to the essential humanity beyond: the best of novelists do this in their writing, though only rarely in their personal lives. The majority of us succumb to more surface impressions. It is hard to sustain a strong sense of equal worth between people whose life experiences are fundamentally different, and all too easy to fall back on self-serving justifications that present the poor as less sensitive to hardship than the wealthy or women as more able to cope with the repetitive tedium of semi-skilled work. Strict equality may not be necessary to sustain equality of worth (given the unlikelihood of achieving such an equality, one can only hope this isn't a necessary condition), but ideals of equal citizenship cannot survive unscathed by great differentials in income and wealth. When the gap between rich and poor opens up too widely, it becomes meaningless to pretend we have recognized all adults as equals.

In the case of gender and race, I have pressed this point further to argue that political equality is incompatible with *any* kind of gap. Some will see this as ridiculously overstated: surely it is

possible for men and women to regard each other as intrinsically
equal even when their life-patterns significantly diverge? Surely
racism can be eradicated without establishing arithmetical equality between white people and black? I cannot prove that my pes-
simism is justified (though current evidence seems mostly on my
side), and will be happy enough if readers just recognize the
legitimacy of the worry. Of course people can be politically
equal even when different. Of course they can be politically
equal even when unequal in some aspects of their lives. There
are none the less certain kinds of inequality and difference that
make a mockery of the political claim. In these cases, it remains
as weird as ever to say that people are equal yet unequal.

Though the explanation lies in the lengthy battles people
fought for their political rights and equalities, it has always aston-
ished me that any elite-ridden, unequal society should have conceded the principle of political equality, when this principle so
invariably generates pressure towards further and deeper equality.
The process of recognizing others as political equals almost always
leads people to question the remaining non-political inequalities.
(Opponents of democracy have long been aware of this phenomenon.) This last – perhaps most important – point about political
equality has even wider ramifications than the economic conditions for the practice of political equality, for inequality begins
to bother people, even when it has no particularly dire effects on
political equalities and rights. Part of what happens in a democratic political culture is that people become impatient with
surrounding inequalities and less willing to put up with what they
perceive as injustice: less prepared to heap rewards on those who
have the talents capitalism currently admires while punishing
those born with a physical disability; less prepared to reward
those born to wealthy parents while punishing those born on the
other side of the tracks. Arbitrariness and unfairness begin to
seem less bearable, less part of the normal fabric of life. At this
point, even inequalities that pose little direct threat to legal, civil
or political equalities begin to come into question.

If this is, as I think, part of the normal evolution of a democratic culture, why then is there such a wall of indifference in
contemporary society, so little questioning of economic inequality today? Not, I believe, because the arguments linking political
with economic equality have become less compelling, but more

for the reasons enshrined in Margaret Thatcher's 'There is no alternative.' The current distribution of income and wealth may be arbitrary, unjust, and at odds with citizen equality, but if we can see no plausible alternative – if, on the contrary, the scope for policy initiatives has been reduced rather than enlarged by the globalization of production and increased vulnerability of national governments that try to buck global trends – we are more inclined just to swallow the injustices. If, in addition, many of the policies that used to be favoured as a means to greater economic equality have come under critical and disparaging scrutiny, there seems little point complaining about remaining inequalities. In an era that has (temporarily) lost sight of the possibilities of economic reorganization and redistribution, it is hardly worth going on about material inequalities. (To adopt another of Thatcher's famous phrases, only the 'moaning minnies' would carry on about these.) In this context, some will shrug off what they none the less perceive as injustice, while others will look for ways of making the paradoxical equality in the midst of inequality seem less so. The importance currently attached to personal responsibility fits well with this last imperative, for it allows us to treat as products of personal 'choice' what an earlier generation might have described as structural inequality. When we no longer feel able to change our circumstances, we would rather believe them equitable and just.

Against this background, it might seem that the real question is not which equalities matter but what (if anything) can be done to make market societies more equal, and that failing serious investigation of alternatives, the arguments I pursue here will have minimal effect. In many ways, I agree with this. However compelling the theoretical connections between political, cultural and economic equality, these have to be combined with evidence about what is viable; and the crucial outstanding questions are about what kind of change is possible within the broad framework of a market economy and what kind of redistribution has worked elsewhere. I make no apology, however, for failing to address these questions, for my main concern is that too little is currently said even about the injustice of economic inequality. If economic equality matters, it is clearly incumbent on social critics to work out the best means of approximating this condition. Against the contemporary wall of indifference, the first task is to establish that case.

Notes

Chapter 1 Democracy and Equality

1 In 1975, 68.7 per cent of the world's countries could be classified as authoritarian, 7.5 per cent as partial democracies, and only 23.8 per cent as liberal democracies. By 1995, the figures were 26.2 per cent, 26.2 per cent and 47.6 per cent. See David Potter, David Goldblatt, Margaret Kiloh and Paul Lewis, *Democratization* (Cambridge, Polity Press/Open University, 1997), p. 9.

2 For obvious reasons, electoral systems that use multi-member constituencies in order to achieve a more proportional representation of the electorate's vote also turn out to be more favourable to the selection of a 'balanced ticket' of women and men.

3 E.g. Michael Sandel, *Democracy's Discontent: America in Search of a Public Philosophy* (Cambridge, Mass., Belknap Press of Harvard University Press, 1996).

4 E.g. Amy Gutmann and Dennis Thompson, *Democracy and Disagreement* (Cambridge, Mass. and London, Belknap Press of Harvard University Press, 1996).

5 E.g. Anne Phillips, *The Politics of Presence* (Oxford, Clarendon Press, 1995).

6 E.g. Will Kymlicka, *Multicultural Citizenship: A Liberal Theory of Minority Rights* (Oxford, Clarendon Press, 1995).

7 Karl Marx, 'On the Jewish Question', in Lucio Colletti (ed.), *Karl Marx: Early Writings* (Harmondsworth, Penguin, 1975).

8 T.H. Marshall, *Citizenship and Social Class and Other Essays* (Cambridge, Cambridge University Press, 1950).

9 E.g. Sidney Verba, Norman H. Nie and Jae-on Kim, *Participation and Political Equality: A Seven Nation Comparison* (Cambridge, Cambridge University Press, 1978).

10 Robert A. Dahl, *Democracy and its Critics* (New Haven, Conn., Yale University Press, 1989).

11 Claus Offe and Ulrich K. Preuss, 'Democratic Institutions and Moral Resources', in David Held (ed.), *Political Theory Today* (Cambridge, Polity Press, 1991).

12 Julian le Grand, *The Strategy for Equality* (London, Allen and Unwin, 1982).

13 This last is one of the themes in Todd Gitlin, *The Twilight of Common Dreams: Why America is Wracked by Culture Wars* (New York, Metropolitan Books/Henry Holt, 1995).

14 Nancy Fraser, *Justice Interruptus: Critical Reflections on the 'Post-socialist' Condition* (London and New York, Routledge, 1997).

15 David Marquand, *The New Reckoning: Capitalism, States and Citizens* (Cambridge, Polity Press, 1997), p. 41.

16 Dahl, *Democracy and its Critics*, p. 97.

17 David Held, *Democracy and the Global Order* (Cambridge, Polity Press, 1995), p. 247.

Chapter 2   Taking Difference Seriously

1 For an example of this last point, see Susan Moller Okin's critique of John Rawls in *Justice, Gender and the Family* (New York, Basic Books, 1989).

2 Kathleen B. Jones, 'Citizenship in a Woman-Friendly Polity', *Signs* 15/4, 1990, p. 784.

3 Carol Gilligan, *In a Different Voice* (Cambridge, Mass., Harvard University Press, 1982).

4 See Patricia J. Williams, *Seeing a Color-Blind Future: The Paradox of Race (Reith Lectures)* (New York, Noonday Press, 1998).

5 See the discussion in Will Kymlicka, *Liberalism, Community and Culture* (Oxford, Clarendon Press, 1989), pp. 142–57.

6 For a fuller discussion of the second issue, see my 'The Politicisation of Difference. Does This Make for a More Intolerant Society?', in John Horton and Susan Mendus (eds), *Toleration, Identity, Difference* (London, Macmillan, 1999).

7 Iris M. Young, *Justice and the Politics of Difference* (Princeton, N.J., Princeton University Press, 1990).

8 Jürgen Habermas, *Between Facts and Norms* (English trans., Cambridge, Polity Press, 1996).

9 Ibid., p. 408.

10 Ibid., p. 408.

11 Ibid., p. 419.

12 Ibid., p. 420.
13 See my *The Politics of Presence* (Oxford, Clarendon Press, 1995).
14 See Jean Bethke Elshtain, *Democracy on Trial* (New York, Basic Books, 1995).
15 Charles Taylor, 'The Politics of Recognition', in Amy Gutmann (ed.), *Multiculturalism and the 'Politics of Recognition'* (Princeton, N.J., Princeton University Press, 1992), p. 59.
16 Iris Young, for example, has explicitly and repeatedly distanced herself from 'essentialist' definitions of what constitutes a group, and employs the Sartrean analogy of a group of people waiting for a bus as a way of talking about the serial – not group – collectivity that constitutes 'women'. See Iris M. Young, 'Gender as Seriality: Thinking About Women as a Social Collective', in her *Intersecting Voices: Dilemmas of Gender, Political Philosophy and Policy* (Princeton, N.J., Princeton University Press, 1997).
17 Diana Coole, 'Is Class a Difference That Makes a Difference?', *Radical Philosophy* 77, 1996, p. 19.
18 See, for example, the essays in David Trend (ed.), *Radical Democracy: Identity, Citizenship and the State* (London and New York, Routledge, 1996).
19 John Rawls, *A Theory of Justice* (Oxford, Oxford University Press, 1971).
20 John Rawls, *Political Liberalism* (New York, Columbia University Press, 1993).

Chapter 3   Does Economic Equality Matter?

1 Thomas Nagel, 'Equality', in *Mortal Questions* (Cambridge, Cambridge University Press, 1979), p. 107.
2 Even this may concede too much to the case for incentives. See G.A. Cohen, *Incentives, Inequality and Community*, Tanner Lectures on Human Values (Stanford, Stanford University Press, 1992).
3 Michael Walzer, *Spheres of Justice* (New York, Basic Books, 1983), p. xii.
4 Ibid., p. xi.
5 Commission on Social Justice, *The Justice Gap* (London, Institute for Public Policy Research, 1993), p. ii.
6 Babeuf, 'Defense', in John Scott (ed.), *The Defense of Gracchus Babeuf* (New York, Schocken Books, 1972), p. 55.
7 Ibid., p. 56.
8 Sylvain Maréchal, 'Manifeste des Egaux', reprinted in Scott, *The Defense of Gracchus Babeuf*, p. 92.

9　Karl Marx, 'Critique of the Gotha Programme', in *Marx and Engels: Selected Works in One Volume* (London, Lawrence and Wishart, 1970), p. 320.
10　John Rawls, *A Theory of Justice* (Oxford, Oxford University Press, 1971), p. 303.
11　Ibid., p. 75.
12　Ibid., p. 303.
13　Ronald Dworkin, 'What is Equality? Part 2: Equality of Resources', *Philosophy and Public Affairs* 10/4, 1981, p. 343.
14　Melanie Phillips, *Observer* 2/11/1997.
15　Michael Young, *The Rise of the Meritocracy: 1870–2033* (London, Thames and Hudson, 1958), p. 124.
16　David Miller, 'Equality', in G.M.K. Hunt (ed.), *Philosophy and Politics* (Cambridge, Cambridge University Press, 1990), p. 86.
17　Amartya Sen, 'Equality of What?', in *Choice, Welfare and Measurement* (Oxford, Blackwell, 1982).
18　Ibid., p. 367.
19　Ronald Dworkin, 'What is Equality? Part 1: Equality of Welfare', *Philosophy and Public Affairs* 10/3, 1981, pp. 185–246.
20　Dworkin, 'What is Equality? Part 2', p. 334.
21　Ibid., p. 295.
22　Ibid., pp. 296–7.
23　Ibid., p. 332.
24　In an argument that draws on the standard economist's account of the market as a device for attaching prices to the very different goods and services we want, Dworkin conjures up a hypothetical auction of resources and a hypothetical insurance market in order to generate a differential distribution of goods that people will none the less recognize as fair. The resulting distribution may include considerable inequalities of money income, but Dworkin sees his analysis as providing a strong defence of progressive taxation. The rich, he argues, cannot be asked to hand over what they have made by their own exertions, but to the extent that they owe their wealth to their good luck in the 'natural' lottery, they can certainly be expected to insure themselves against the risks of not being the kind of people they are. The poor, by contrast, have little to lose by being any different, and can hardly be expected to pay out on taxation/insurance.
25　One seeming qualification to this is that in the initial auction of resources (on Dworkin's hypothetical desert island), everyone has a strictly equal number of clamshells. Dworkin then builds in the necessary complexity to allow for the different values we attach to different goods, but in his starting point at least he still operates with a simple division of the world's resources.

26 Dworkin, 'What is Equality? Part 2', p. 343.
27 Will Kymlicka, *Contemporary Political Philosophy* (Oxford, Clarendon Press, 1990), pp. 73–4.
28 David Miller, 'What Kind of Equality Should the Left Pursue?', in Jane Franklin (ed.), *Equality* (London, Institute for Public Policy Research, 1997), p. 189.
29 Amartya Sen, 'Work, Needs, and Inequality', in *On Economic Inequality* (Oxford, Clarendon Press, 1997), pp. 104–5.
30 Harry Frankfurt, 'Equality as a Moral Ideal', *Ethics* 98, 1987, p. 21.
31 Joseph Raz, *The Morality of Freedom* (Oxford, Clarendon Press, 1986), ch. 9.
32 Sen, *On Economic Inequality*, p. 213.
33 Walzer, *Spheres of Justice*.
34 Ibid., p. 20.
35 E.g. Richard J. Arneson, 'Against "Complex" Equality', in David Miller and Michael Walzer (eds), *Pluralism, Justice and Equality* (Oxford, Oxford University Press, 1995).
36 Walzer, *Spheres of Justice*, p. xiii.
37 Michael Walzer, 'Exclusion, Injustice and the Democratic State', *Dissent* Winter, 1993.
38 Walzer, *Spheres of Justice*, p. 213.
39 Robert Nozick, *Anarchy, State and Utopia* (Oxford, Blackwell, 1974).

Chapter 4   From Access to Recognition

1 This was a key part of Carole Pateman's argument in *Participation and Democratic Theory* (Cambridge, Cambridge University Press, 1970).
2 Geraint Parry, George Moyser and Neil Day, *Political Participation and Democracy in Britain* (Cambridge, Cambridge University Press, 1992), p. 84.
3 Ibid., ch. 4.
4 Philip Green, *Retrieving Democracy: In Search of Civic Equality* (London, Methuen, 1985).
5 This is one of the conclusions I take from Parry et al., *Political Participation and Democracy in Britain*.
6 Charles Taylor, 'The Politics of Recognition', in Amy Gutmann (ed.), *Multiculturalism and the 'Politics of Recognition'* (Princeton, N.J., Princeton University Press, 1992), p. 38.
7 Desmond S. King and Jeremy Waldron, 'Citizenship, Social Citizenship and the Defence of Welfare Provision', *British Journal of Political Science* 18/4, 1988, p. 443.

8 David Miller, 'What Kind of Equality Should the Left Pursue?', in Jane Franklin (ed.), *Equality* (London, Institute for Public Policy Research, 1997), p. 94.

9 Richard Rorty, *Contingency, irony and solidarity* (Cambridge, Cambridge University Press, 1989), p. 192.

10 Tariq Modood, Richard Berthond, Jane Lakey, James Nazroo, Patten Smith, Satnam Virdee and Sharon Beishon, *Ethnic Minorities in Britain: Diversity and Disadvantage* (London, Policy Studies Institute, 1997).

11 Judith Butler, 'Merely Cultural', *Social Text* 15/2&3, 1997.

12 This is central to Butler's critique of Fraser in 'Merely Cultural'.

13 Fraser identifies these as the two moves in Judith Butler's argument against viewing homosexuality as 'merely cultural'. Nancy Fraser, 'Heterosexism, Misrecognition, and Capitalism: A Response to Judith Butler', *Social Text* 15/2&3, 1997.

14 Nancy Fraser, *Justice Interruptus: Critical Reflections on the 'Post-socialist' Condition* (London and New York, Routledge, 1997), p. 15.

15 Fraser, 'Heterosexism, Misrecognition, and Capitalism', p. 281.

16 Ibid., p. 285.

17 Fraser, *Justice Interruptus*, p. 29.

18 Sheldon Wolin, 'The Liberal/Democratic Divide: On Rawls's Political Liberalism', *Political Theory* 245/1, 1996, p. 101.

Chapter 5   Deliberation and the Republic

1 Hence the deep disquiet when political scientists come up with what seem like 'laws of political behaviour' to mirror the 'laws of nature' or the 'laws of economic science', as with Robert Michels's suggestion that all political organizations, including those that seem most committed to principles of internal democracy, fall prey to an 'iron law of oligarchy' that inevitably distances them from their founding beliefs.

2 Sheldon Wolin, *Politics and Vision* (Boston, Little, Brown, 1960), p. 431.

3 Ibid., pp. 293–4.

4 Jean Bethke Elshtain, *Public Man, Private Woman: Women in Social and Political Thought* (Princeton, N.J., Princeton University Press, 1981), p. 301.

5 See the readings collected in Joan Landes (ed.), *Feminism and the Public Sphere* (Oxford, Oxford University Press, 1998).

6 This is a central division between Jean Bethke Elshtain and Mary Dietz. See Jean Bethke Elshtain, 'Antigone's Daughters', and Mary

G. Dietz, 'Context is All: Feminism and Theories of Citizenship', both reprinted in Anne Phillips (ed.), *Feminism and Politics* (Oxford, Oxford University Press, 1998).

7 See Ruth Lister, *Citizenship: Feminist Perspectives* (London, Macmillan, 1997).

8 Hannah Arendt, *On Revolution* (London, Faber and Faber, 1963), p. 54.

9 Ibid., p. 137.

10 Totalitarianism, in Arendt's view, expressed a uniquely modern mixture of determinism and 'everything is possible'. Surrendering themselves to what they saw as irreversible forces, totalitarian regimes abdicated responsibility for human action and choice. But they combined this with the belief that anything is possible if one only sides with the forces of necessity: 'reckless optimism' combined with 'reckless despair' (*The Origins of Totalitarianism*, London, George Allen and Unwin, 1961, p. xxix). Though uneasy at finding herself in the same camp with those 'professional anti-Marxists' (*The Human Condition*, Chicago, University of Chicago Press, 1958, p. 79) whose motivation she deplored, Arendt believed that Marxism had contributed significantly to this denial of political life. The point about Marx was not that he saw the course of history as determined by forces beyond human control; the point, rather, is that he treated the making of history as if it were analogous to the making of objects. Just as the carpenter had to work with the laws of nature in order to transform recalcitrant material into the desired object, so too were human beings to work with the laws of history in order to wrest their desired future from the wreckage of contemporary life. Encouraging us to think that we 'make' history (rather than acting in it), historical materialism led us to think of freedom as a matter of siding with natural laws. It also led into the moral abdication that sees the ends justifying the means, for if history is made on the model of carpentry, we can hardly be surprised if we have to wreak violence on our material before transforming it into something else. This betrayal of political responsibility contributed significantly, Arendt argued, to the emergence of totalitarianism.

11 Benjamin Barber, *Strong Democracy* (Berkeley, Calif., University of California Press, 1984).

12 Michael Sandel, *Democracy's Discontent: America in Search of a Public Philosophy* (Cambridge, Mass., Belknap Press of Harvard University Press, 1996), p. 26.

13 Ibid., pp. 325–8.

14 Ibid., p. 333.

15 This is very clear in Benjamin Barber's *Strong Democracy*, where he takes issue with 'unitary' conceptions of democracy and stresses the plurality of modern society.
16 Iris M. Young, 'Polity and Group Difference: A Critique of the Ideal of Universal Citizenship', *Ethics* 9, 1989.
17 Jürgen Habermas, *Between Facts and Norms* (English trans., Cambridge, Polity Press, 1996), p. 309.
18 Sheldon Wolin, *The Presence of the Past: Essays on the State and the Constitution* (Baltimore and London, Johns Hopkins University Press, 1989), pp. 4–5.
19 Philip Pettit, *Republicanism: A Theory of Freedom and Government* (Oxford, Clarendon Press, 1997).
20 Lydia Becker, organizer of the Manchester Suffrage Society from the 1860s to the 1880s, quoted in Andrew Rosen, *Rise Up Women!* (London, Routledge and Kegan Paul, 1974), p. 8.
21 Pettit, *Republicanism*, p. 78.
22 Habermas's much-repeated formulation is that only those norms are valid 'to which all possibly affected persons could agree as participants in rational discourses'. See *Between Facts and Norms*, p. 107.
23 Barber, *Strong Democracy*.
24 Jane Mansbridge, 'A Deliberative Theory of Interest Representation', in M.P. Pettraca (ed.), *The Politics of Interests* (Boulder, Colo., Westview Press, 1992), p. 37.
25 Claus Offe and Ulrich K. Preuss, 'Democratic Institutions and Moral Resources', in David Held (ed.), *Political Theory Today* (Cambridge, Polity Press, 1991), pp. 156–7.
26 E.g. Amy Gutmann and Dennis Thompson, 'Moral Conflict and Political Consensus', *Ethics* 101, 1990; Jürgen Habermas, 'Struggles for Recognition in Constitutional States', *European Journal of Philosophy* 1/2, 1993; Iris M. Young, 'Justice and Communicative Democracy', in R. Gottlieb (ed.), *Tradition, Counter-Tradition, Politics: Dimensions of Radical Philosophy* (Philadelphia, Temple University Press, 1994).
27 This is one of the key ideas developed by James Fishkin, *Deliberation and Democracy: New Directions for Democratic Reform* (Yale University Press, 1991).
28 Iris M. Young, 'Justice and Communicative Democracy', in R. Gottlieb (ed.), *Tradition, Counter-Tradition, Politics: Dimensions of Radical Philosophy* (Philadelphia, Temple University Press, 1994); Iris M. Young, 'Communication and the Other: Beyond Deliberative Democracy', in S. Benhabib (ed.), *Democracy and Difference: Contesting the Boundaries of the Political* (Princeton, N.J., Princeton University Press, 1996).

29 Cass Sunstein, 'Preferences and Politics', *Philosophy and Public Affairs* 20/1, 1991, p. 34.
30 Gutmann and Thompson, 'Moral Conflict and Political Consensus', p. 154.
31 Amy Gutmann and Dennis Thompson, *Democracy and Disagreement* (Cambridge, Mass. and London, Belknap Press of Harvard University Press, 1996), p. 83.
32 Jane J. Mansbridge, 'The Rise and Fall of Self Interest in the Explanation of Political Life', in Jane J. Mansbridge (ed.), *Beyond Self Interest* (Chicago, Chicago University Press, 1990), p. 21.
33 Germaine Greer, *The Female Eunuch* (London, Paladin, 1970), p. 328.
34 David Estlund, 'Who's Afraid of Deliberative Democracy? On the Strategic/Deliberative Dichotomy in Recent Constitutional Jurisprudence', *Texas Law Review* 71/1, 1993.
35 Sunstein, 'Preferences and Politics', p. 4.

Chapter 6   Equal Yet Unequal?

1 Hilary Mantel, 'Review of Dominique Godineau: The Women of Paris and Their French Revolution', *London Review of Books* 20/14, 16 July 1998.
2 Will Kymlicka, *Multicultural Citizenship: A Liberal Theory of Minority Rights* (Oxford, Clarendon Press, 1995), p. 1.
3 Hannah Arendt, *The Human Condition* (Chicago, University of Chicago Press, 1958).
4 Though I do not address this here, they would also include free access to public media of communication so as to ensure under-resourced campaign groups an effective voice.

Bibliography

Arendt, Hannah, *The Human Condition* (Chicago, University of Chicago Press, 1958).

Arendt, Hannah, *The Origins of Totalitarianism* (London, George Allen and Unwin, 1961).

Arendt, Hannah, *On Revolution* (London, Faber and Faber, 1963).

Arneson, Richard J., 'Against "Complex" Equality', in David Miller and Michael Walzer (eds), *Pluralism, Justice and Equality* (Oxford, Oxford University Press, 1995).

Babeuf, Gracchus, 'Defense', in John Scott (ed.), *The Defense of Gracchus Babeuf* (New York, Schocken Books, 1972).

Barber, Benjamin, *Strong Democracy* (Berkeley, Calif., University of California Press, 1984).

Butler, Judith, 'Merely Cultural', *Social Text* 15/2&3, 1997.

Cohen, G.A., *Incentives, Inequality and Community*, Tanner Lectures on Human Values (Stanford, Stanford University Press, 1992).

Cohen, G.A., 'Back to Socialist Basics', in Jane Franklin (ed.), *Equality* (London, Institute for Public Policy Research, 1997).

Commission on Social Justice, *The Justice Gap* (London, Institute for Public Policy Research, 1993).

Coole, Diana, 'Is Class a Difference That Makes a Difference?', *Radical Philosophy* 77, 1996.

Dahl, Robert A., *Democracy and its Critics* (New Haven, Conn., Yale University Press, 1989).

Dietz, Mary G., 'Context is All: Feminism and Theories of Citizenship', reprinted in Anne Phillips (ed.), *Feminism and Politics* (Oxford, Oxford University Press, 1998).

Dworkin, Ronald, 'What is Equality? Part 1: Equality of Welfare', *Philosophy and Public Affairs* 10/3, 1981.

Dworkin, Ronald, 'What is Equality? Part 2: Equality of Resources', *Philosophy and Public Affairs* 10/4, 1981.

Elshtain, Jean Bethke, *Public Man, Private Woman: Women in Social and Political Thought* (Princeton, N.J., Princeton University Press, 1981).

Elshtain, Jean Bethke, *Democracy on Trial* (New York, Basic Books, 1995).

Elshtain, Jean Bethke, 'Antigone's Daughters', reprinted in Anne Phillips (ed.), *Feminism and Politics* (Oxford, Oxford University Press, 1998).

Estlund, David, 'Who's Afraid of Deliberative Democracy? On the Strategic/Deliberative Dichotomy in Recent Constitutional Jurisprudence', *Texas Law Review* 71/1, 1993.

Fishkin, James, *Deliberation and Democracy: New Directions for Democratic Reform* (New Haven, Conn., Yale University Press, 1991).

Frankfurt, Harry, 'Equality as a Moral Ideal', *Ethics* 98, 1987.

Fraser, Nancy, *Justice Interruptus: Critical Reflections on the 'Postsocialist' Condition* (London and New York, Routledge, 1997).

Fraser, Nancy, 'Heterosexism, Misrecognition, and Capitalism: A Response to Judith Butler', *Social Text* 15/2&3, 1997.

Gilligan, Carol, *In a Different Voice* (Cambridge, Mass., Harvard University Press, 1982).

Gitlin, Todd, *The Twilight of Common Dreams: Why America is Wracked by Culture Wars* (New York, Metropolitan Books/Henry Holt, 1995).

Green, Philip, *Retrieving Democracy: In Search of Civic Equality* (London, Methuen, 1985).

Greer, Germaine, *The Female Eunuch* (London, Paladin, 1970).

Gutmann, Amy, *Liberal Equality* (Cambridge, Cambridge University Press, 1980).

Gutmann, Amy (ed.), *Multiculturalism and the 'Politics of Recognition'* (Princeton, N.J., Princeton University Press, 1992).

Gutmann, Amy and Dennis Thompson, 'Moral Conflict and Political Consensus' *Ethics* 101, 1990.

Gutmann, Amy and Dennis Thompson, *Democracy and Disagreement* (Cambridge, Mass. and London, Belknap Press of Harvard University Press, 1996).

Habermas, Jürgen, 'Struggles for Recognition in Constitutional States', *European Journal of Philosophy* 1/2, 1993.

Habermas, Jürgen, *Between Facts and Norms* (English trans., Cambridge, Polity Press, 1996).

Held, David, *Democracy and the Global Order* (Cambridge, Polity Press, 1995).

Hirst, Paul, *Associative Democracy* (Cambridge, Polity Press, 1994).

Jones, Kathleen B., 'Citizenship in a Woman-Friendly Polity', *Signs* 15/4, 1990.

King, Desmond S. and Jeremy Waldron, 'Citizenship, Social Citizenship and the Defence of Welfare Provision', *British Journal of Political Science* 18/4, 1988.

Kymlicka, Will, *Liberalism, Community and Culture* (Oxford, Clarendon Press, 1989).

Kymlicka, Will, *Contemporary Political Philosophy* (Oxford, Clarendon Press, 1990).

Kymlicka, Will, *Multicultural Citizenship: A Liberal Theory of Minority Rights* (Oxford, Clarendon Press, 1995).

Landes, Joan (ed.), *Feminism and the Public Sphere* (Oxford, Oxford University Press, 1998).

le Grand, Julian, *The Strategy for Equality* (London, Allen and Unwin, 1982).

Lister, Ruth, *Citizenship: Feminist Perspectives* (London, Macmillan, 1997).

Mansbridge, Jane J., 'The Rise and Fall of Self Interest in the Explanation of Political Life', in Jane J. Mansbridge (ed.), *Beyond Self Interest* (Chicago, University of Chicago Press, 1990).

Mansbridge, Jane J., 'A Deliberative Theory of Interest Representation', in M.P. Pettraca (ed.), *The Politics of Interests* (Boulder, Colo., Westview Press, 1992).

Maréchal, Sylvain, 'Manifeste des Egaux', reprinted in John Scott (ed.), *The Defense of Gracchus Babeuf* (New York, Schocken Books, 1972).

Marquand, David, *The New Reckoning: Capitalism, States and Citizens* (Cambridge, Polity Press, 1997).

Marshall, T.H., *Citizenship and Social Class and Other Essays* (Cambridge, Cambridge University Press, 1950).

Marx, Karl, 'Critique of the Gotha Programme', in *Marx and Engels: Selected Works in One Volume* (London, Lawrence and Wishart, 1970).

Marx, Karl, *Capital: Volume I* (London, Lawrence and Wishart, 1970).

Marx, Karl, 'On the Jewish Question', in Lucio Colletti (ed.), *Karl Marx: Early Writings* (Harmondsworth, Penguin, 1975).

Miller, David, 'Equality', in G.M.K. Hunt (ed.), *Philosophy and Politics* (Cambridge, Cambridge University Press, 1990).

Miller, David. 'What Kind of Equality Should the Left Pursue?', in Jane Franklin (ed.), *Equality* (London, Institute for Public Policy Research, 1997).

Miller, David and Michael Walzer (eds), *Pluralism, Justice and Equality* (Oxford, Oxford University Press, 1995).

Modood, Tariq, Richard Berthond, Jane Lakey, James Nazroo, Patten Smith, Satnam Virdee and Sharon Beishon, *Ethnic Minorities in Britain: Diversity and Disadvantage* (London, Policy Studies Institute, 1997).

Moller Okin, Susan, *Justice, Gender and the Family* (New York, Basic Books, 1989).

Nagel, Thomas, 'Equality', in Thomas Nagel *Mortal Questions* (Cambridge, Cambridge University Press, 1979).

Nozick, Robert, *Anarchy, State and Utopia* (Oxford, Blackwell, 1974).

Offe, Claus and Ulrich K. Preuss, 'Democratic Institutions and Moral Resources', in David Held (ed.), *Political Theory Today* (Cambridge, Polity Press, 1991).

Parry, Geraint, George Moyser and Neil Day, *Political Participation and Democracy in Britain* (Cambridge, Cambridge University Press, 1992).

Pateman, Carole, *Participation and Democratic Theory* (Cambridge, Cambridge University Press, 1970).

Pettit, Philip, *Republicanism: A Theory of Freedom and Government* (Oxford, Clarendon Press, 1997).

Phillips, Anne, *The Politics of Presence* (Oxford, Clarendon Press, 1995).

Phillips, Anne (ed.), *Feminism and Politics* (Oxford, Oxford University Press, 1998).

Phillips, Anne, 'The Politicisation of Difference. Does This Make for a More Intolerant Society?', in John Horton and Susan Mendus (eds), *Toleration, Identity, Difference* (London, Macmillan, 1999).

Potter, David, David Goldblatt, Margaret Kiloh and Paul Lewis, *Democratization* (Cambridge, Polity Press/Open University, 1997).

Rawls, John, *A Theory of Justice* (Oxford, Oxford University Press, 1971).

Rawls, John, *Political Liberalism* (New York, Columbia University Press, 1993).

Raz, Joseph, *The Morality of Freedom* (Oxford, Clarendon Press, 1986).

Rorty, Richard, *Contingency, irony and solidarity* (Cambridge, Cambridge University Press, 1989).

Rosen, Andrew, *Rise Up Women!* (London, Routledge and Kegan Paul, 1974).

Sandel, Michael, *Democracy's Discontent: America in Search of a Public Philosophy* (Cambridge, Mass., Belknap Press of Harvard University Press, 1996).

Sen, Amartya, 'Equality of What?', in Amartya Sen *Choice, Welfare and Measurement* (Oxford, Blackwell, 1982).

Sen, Amartya, 'Work, Needs, and Inequality', in Amartya Sen *On Economic Inequality* (Oxford, Clarendon Press, 1997).

Sunstein, Cass, 'Preferences and Politics', *Philosophy and Public Affairs* 20/1, 1991.

Taylor, Charles, 'The Politics of Recognition', in Amy Gutmann (ed.), *Multiculturalism and the 'Politics of Recognition'* (Princeton, N.J., Princeton University Press, 1992).

Trend, David (ed.), *Radical Democracy: Identity, Citizenship and the State* (London and New York, Routledge, 1996).

Verba, Sidney, Norman H. Nie and Jae-on Kim, *Participation and Political Equality: A Seven Nation Comparison* (Cambridge, Cambridge University Press, 1978).

Walzer, Michael, *Spheres of Justice* (New York, Basic Books, 1983).

Walzer, Michael, 'Exclusion, Injustice and the Democratic State', *Dissent* Winter, 1993.

Williams, Patricia J., *Seeing a Color-Blind Future: The Paradox of Race (Reith Lectures)* (New York, Noonday Press, 1998).

Wolin, Sheldon, *Politics and Vision* (Boston, Little and Brown, 1960).

Wolin, Sheldon, *The Presence of the Past: Essays on the State and the Constitution* (Baltimore and London, Johns Hopkins University Press, 1989).

Wolin, Sheldon, 'The Liberal/Democratic Divide: On Rawls's Political Liberalism', *Political Theory* 245/1, 1996.

Young, Iris M., 'Polity and Group Difference: A Critique of the Ideal of Universal Citizenship', *Ethics* 9, 1989.

Young, Iris M., *Justice and the Politics of Difference* (Princeton, N.J., Princeton University Press, 1990).

Young, Iris M., 'Justice and Communicative Democracy', in R. Gottlieb (ed.), *Tradition, Counter-Tradition, Politics: Dimensions of Radical Philosophy* (Philadelphia, Temple University Press, 1994).

Young, Iris M., 'Communication and the Other: Beyond Deliberative Democracy', in S. Benhabib (ed.), *Democracy and Difference: Contesting the Boundaries of the Political* (Princeton, N.J., Princeton University Press, 1996).

Young, Iris M., 'Gender as Seriality: Thinking About Women as a Social Collective', in *Intersecting Voices: Dilemmas of Gender, Political Philosophy and Policy* (Princeton, N.J., Princeton University Press, 1997).

Young, Michael, *The Rise of the Meritocracy: 1870–2033* (London, Thames and Hudson, 1958).

Index

choice
  and equality of opportunity 51,
    55–60, 68, 69
  and non-domination 57, 111
  and politics 100, 102
  rational 44
  and structural inequality 58,
    75, 133
  see also preference
citizenship
  and citizen's initiative 6, 9
  and citizens' juries 117
  and civic republicanism 106–9
  and difference 9, 14, 26–7
  and economic equality 15, 98
  and equality of worth 2, 80,
    106, 131
  and feminism 22, 23, 103
  and liberal democracy 99,
    101–2
  and minorities 1, 127–8
  multicultural 1, 5, 85, 89, 116,
    120
  and participatory democracy
    8–9, 74–7, 80, 104, 111
  and political equality 2–3, 10,
    75, 90, 127
  and the public sphere 99,
    101–3, 108–9
  and recognition 84, 98, 120
  and social equality 8, 31
  and suffrage 3, 7, 8, 16, 21, 27,
    79, 123, 124
  and welfare rights 80
civil rights movement 20–1
civil society
  and the state 7
  see also equality, civil;
    republicanism, civic
class
  and civic republicanism 108
  and economic/cultural
    domination 87–8

  and equality 10, 13–14, 20–1,
    26, 73, 76–8, 98
  and hegemony of difference 42
  and occupation 77
  and power relations 47, 90
  solidarities 13, 108
  and state 88
clitoridectomy, ban on 27, 38
Commission on Social Justice 45
communism, collapse 11, 20
communitarianism
  and civic republicanism 106–8
  and tradition 115
comparison, and equality 61–2, 72
Comte, A. 101
condition, equality of 94–5, 127
constitution, reform 4–5, 9
convergence
  and assimilationism 90–6, 128
  cultural 86, 91–4, 96, 97
  and difference 19, 86, 90–6,
    128
  economic 11–12, 85–6, 90–1,
    95
Coole, Diana 42
corporatism, and group
    representation 40
Crosland, Anthony 15
culture
  and convergence 86, 91–4, 96,
    97
  of dependency 12, 106
  and domination 9, 13, 84–90,
    91–4, 127
  and equality 20, 25, 107
  'men's' 93
  minority 1, 3, 9, 36, 38, 85
  'women's' 92–4
  working-class 42

Dahl, Robert A. 8, 15
democracy
  and capitalism 17–18, 77

elections, competitive 8, 124–5
Elshtain, Jean Bethke 102
empowerment
  and economic equality 14
  and political equality 32, 75
  and social equality 15, 31
entitlement, universal 12, 80, 83
envy 61, 62, 79
equality
  and difference 5, 9, 14, 18–19,
    23–43, 96–8, 127–9
  and inequality 2, 124–33
  of worth *see* worth
equality, civil 21–2, 26–7, 105
equality, economic 44–73
  and access to politics 74–9, 83, 85
  complex 64–8
  and convergence 11–12, 85–6,
    90–1, 95
  definition 16
  and democracy vii, 1, 6–18, 43,
    82, 99–123: deliberative
    113–16, 123; liberal 18, 19,
    27, 99–100
  and domination 57, 64–6,
    86–90, 112–13
  and equality of worth 81–3,
    94, 98, 131
  importance 1, 7–8, 68–73, 74,
    98, 132–3
  and politics of difference 18,
    27, 30, 33–5, 42–3
  and resource distribution 52–4,
    87
  retreat from 51–4
  revisionist views 44–5
  simple 45–51, 53, 56, 58,
    64–5, 66, 68: and income
    inequalities 12–13, 45–8, 71,
    131
  and social equality 30–2
  and sufficiency 60–4, 66, 72,
    80

  see also equality, political;
    income inequalities; resources
equality, gender *see* equality,
  sexual; gender
equality, legal 124
  and difference 25–6, 27, 30, 36
equality of opportunity
  and choice 51, 55–60, 68, 69
  and income inequality 2, 13,
    18, 49, 50, 55
  and social mobility 78
equality, political
  and access 74–9, 80, 83, 85
  and capitalism 7–8, 10, 17–18,
    132
  and citizenship 2–3
  and civic republicanism 107
  critique 6–10, 125
  and democracy 1–5, 6–10, 16,
    34–5, 82–3
  and difference 9, 14, 20, 27,
    30–5, 40, 85, 132
  and economic equality 6–19,
    20–1, 62, 72–3, 125–6: and
    access 74–9, 83; and
    deliberation 123; and
    democracy 1–2; and
    difference 27, 30, 33–5,
    42–3, 98; and freedom as
    non-domination 111–12; and
    inequalities 130; and liberal
    democracy 18, 19, 27,
    99–105
  and equality of worth 15–16,
    79–83, 97, 131
  importance 124–5
  and inequality 129–30
  and social equality 2, 6, 8–9,
    12, 15–16, 33–5, 110
  and substantive equality 6,
    7–8, 124–33
equality, racial 1
  and difference 26

property, private
  and inequality 2, 7, 17, 20, 46, 127
  and political rights 3, 75, 123
Proudhon, Pierre Joseph 101

quota systems 30, 33–4, 117, 130

race
  and economic/cultural domination 87, 89, 95–6
  and neutrality 24–5
  and political equality 3, 5, 90, 126, 131–2
  and politics of difference 42, 89, 95–6
racism
  and deliberative democracy 116, 122
  discreditation 1, 20–1, 132
  and economic inequality 85–6, 89
  neglect 120
radicalism, social 112–13, 123
Rawls, John 43, 48–50, 54, 56, 63, 70, 79
Raz, Joseph 61
recognition
  and egalitarianism 13, 29, 39–40, 42
  and gender 93, 94–5
  and misrecognition 84–90, 120
  and political equality 78, 80, 83, 85, 92, 132
  and tolerance 18, 27–8
referenda 6, 9
reform
  constitutional 4–5, 9, 14
  economic 9, 11, 124, 130
  political 6, 8, 30
  social 124
religion
  and civic republicanism 108

and convergence 91, 96–7
  and political equality 7, 84, 90
  and the state 7, 84
representation
  'group' 5, 10, 40–1, 118
  inequalities 75
  of minorities 5, 9, 21, 30, 32–3, 37, 40–1, 85, 117, 127
  proportional 4–5, 9, 117
  of women 5, 9, 22, 24, 33–4, 37, 41, 95, 117–18, 126
republicanism
  civic 5, 15, 105–11
  and freedom as non-domination 111–13
  and social radicalism 112–13, 123
resources, economic 60, 68, 72, 120
  and sufficiency 60–4, 80
resources, political, distribution 8, 74, 80, 83, 87
resources, social 15, 52–4, 55, 63, 66, 120
respect, equality of 79, 83, 85–7, 91–6, 97–8, 119, 128
  and tolerance 27–8, 107, 125
responsibility
  civic 106, 109–20
  ethic of 24
  individual 12–13, 51, 55, 58–60, 68, 133
  political 104
rights, and duties 107
Rorty, Richard 81
Rousseau, Jean-Jacques 79, 103, 105

Sandel, Michael 105–7
Schumpeter, Joseph 45
secularism, and religious minorities 84